Speaking, Listening and Understanding

Speaking, Listening and Understanding

Debate for Non–Native-English Speakers

Gary Rybold

International Debate Education Association
New York · Amsterdam · Brussels

Published by
International Debate Education Association
400 West 59th Street
New York, NY 10019

For permission to reproduce in whole or in part, please contact: idea@ idebate.org

Library of Congress Cataloging-in-Publication Data

Rybold, Gary.
  Speaking, Listening and Understanding : debate for non–native-English speakers / Gary Rybold.
    p. cm.
  ISBN-13: 978-1-932716-24-5
  ISBN-10: 1-932716-24-6
  1. Debates and debating. 2. English language—Study and teaching—Foreign speakers. I. Title.
  PN4181.R94 2006
  808.5'3—dc22

IDEBATE Press Books

To Xiaoqing, whose love inspires me

Contents

Preface

Speaking, Listening and Understanding introduces new English language speakers to the basics of debate. The initial version of this text was presented at the International Debate Festival held at the Xi'an International Studies University in the People's Republic of China in August 2004. Before writing this book, I noticed that there were no simple debate texts for new English language students. Texts available in the United States seemed too complex or used excessive cultural references. Too often, these qualities made learning difficult. This text was written with the non–native-English speakers in mind.

I had my first debate in 1965. Since that time I have met thousands of people who have found that the world of debate opened the doors of knowledge. At the heart of debate is a sharing of ideas and information. Ultimately, this book is about that sharing. I will share information that should help you get started in formal debating. Then once you debate, you will share your ideas on a variety of topics. As you share, you will also learn new concepts, a new vocabulary, and a love for the exchange of ideas.

Different coaches have different theories about debate. As you develop as a debater, you will learn these. Like all theories, some you may like and others you may not. Part of the sharing process in debate involves understanding how others see the world.

I would also like you to share your experiences in learning debate. If you read something in this book that is unclear or if you would like to see something added, I encourage you to write to me. Please send all recommendations and comments through IDEA at www.idebate.org. I feel honored to be part of your learning experience and would appreciate any ideas you have. Good luck and good debating.

Gary Rybold
Irvine Valley College
Irvine, California

Chapters in Brief

Speaking, Listening and Understanding was written to make it easier for you to become a debater. Each chapter is short enough to read in one session. At the end of each chapter, you will find a list of the important concepts and key vocabulary terms used in that chapter. All definitions are listed in the glossary at the end of the book. Each chapter teaches you a skill, which the next chapter builds on.

Chapter 1 welcomes you to debate and encourages you to be the best student of communication that you can be. Remember, the skills you learn should help you in every language, not just English.

Chapter 2 explains the basic concepts of debate. You will learn some of the rules and responsibilities of debate and what you should do when you participate.

Chapter 3 explains how to improve your oral skills (delivery). It also helps you overcome any fear of public speaking you might have.

Chapter 4 discusses how to write clear speeches and papers.

Chapter 5 describes the many different debate formats. Debates can be held with different time limits, types of questions, and number of debaters. The chapter also includes the time limits used for debate formats in the United States.

Chapter 6 discusses different types of propositions—how topics are worded to make them easier to debate.

Chapter 7 describes how to develop cases. Cases are how you write organized arguments to support your side.

Chapter 8 discusses critical thinking. You will learn how to understand the parts of an argument and how to tell when someone is using thinking that is not logical (using fallacies).

Chapter 9 discusses research. It explains how to find evidence to support your arguments, how to use the evidence in the debate, and how to attack the evidence of the other team.

Chapter 10 explains refutation. You will learn how to defeat the arguments of the other side and how to defend your own.

Chapter 11 explains note taking and "flowing" for debate. You will learn how to flow the arguments in a debate.

Chapter 12 describes tournaments and judging. You will learn how a tournament works and the different approaches that judges take in their evaluations.

CHAPTER 1

Welcome to Debate

This chapter introduces the activity of debating and explains skills that you will gain if you participate in debates often. In choosing to read this book, you are now a student of communication. *Speaking, Listening and Understanding* covers a special kind of communication: U.S. style debate. So, if you want to improve your presentation skills and your critical thinking abilities, read on! Although debating is a great educational opportunity, let me start off with a simple statement:

People debate because it is FUN.

Debating Teaches Skills

Public Speaking

I know that most people have a fear of public speaking. In fact, in my classes, I start the first day by telling my students that speaking before an audience is the number one fear in the United States. Death is only seventh on the list. That means more people would rather die than get up to speak in front of a group. Yet, the thousands of debaters I have debated, taught, coached, and judged have learned to love public speaking. Once they get over their fears, the excitement of competition becomes more enjoyable with each debate. And debaters know they are developing skills that will help them for the rest of their lives. For this reason, many English teachers use debate as an effective way to teach speaking skills.

When you first started learning English, you probably began with grammar rules. Often, students learn to read and write English before they practice their *oral* (speaking) skills. If this happened to you, speaking in English may not be as easy as writing in English. You may even be so shy that you do not want to share your ideas. Debating will help you overcome your fears and develop your oral English skills. In fact, debating is like an immersion program: eventually, you will begin thinking in English!

Debating will help you to become a better speaker in all situations—private and public. Everyone in the debate contributes and has a voice in the argumentation. With new debating skills, you will be able to give more power to your own voice.

Of course, you will make mistakes. All debaters do. That is why debating is something you must practice. As you practice thinking about your ideas and explaining those ideas to others, you will gain confidence, and you will express your ideas more clearly when you speak.

Debate also develops several other skills that will help you communicate effectively in English—or in any language you use.

Critical Thinking

Critical thinking skills are important not only in debate but also in other aspects of your life. Critical thinking helps you to ask better questions, evaluate answers, keep an open mind, be honest about your own biases, and make better decisions. You can improve several critical thinking skills by studying debate:

1. Debate will teach you how to use reliable sources of information. Not all information is good. You will learn how to evaluate sources to find those that are most reliable and most valuable. You will gather evidence from many sources and assess and compare their arguments.

2. Debate will teach you how to develop good arguments and find the flaws in bad arguments. Arguments can be strong or weak. You will learn to present the best arguments for your side and understand the weaknesses of your own and others' arguments.

3. Debate will teach you how to solve problems. One of the main reasons for debating is to find solutions to problems. You will learn how to make comparisons and determine the best solutions.

4. Debate will teach you how to ask and answer questions. When debaters learn to ask questions, they can determine the central points of an issue. When they respond to questions, they clarify their own thinking.

Other Skills

1. **Note Taking:** Debate will help you to become a better note taker. Since your debates may last an hour or more, you will need to write down what the other team says, what your partner says, and even what you want to say. You will be surprised how your memory will improve at the same time.

2. **Organizing:** Debate will help you to become a better organizer. Because each of your debates will involve many ideas, you must be able to organize them so that the audience understands your arguments and how each one fits into the debate.

3. **Researching:** Debate will help you become a better researcher. To be successful in debate, you need to understand both sides of an issue and support your position with evidence. You will learn how to use libraries and electronic resources to find the information you need. You will also learn how to evaluate material and organize it efficiently.

4. **Writing:** Debate will help you to become a better writer. Once you complete your research, you must be able to write speeches, or *briefs*, short organized arguments that help you to understand and explain your viewpoint.

5. **Listening:** Debate will help you to become a better listener. When members of the other team are speaking, you must listen to what they say so that you can respond. In many debates you will have a partner. You will also have to listen to him or her carefully in order to advance your

side. You will become a *critical listener*, which means that you will think about what is being said.

6. **Teamwork and People Skills**: Debate will teach you teamwork and *people skills* because you must work and think as a team in order to succeed. You will have to work with a partner, coach, and other teammates, sharing information and developing strategies. As you develop your speaking skills, you will also develop your people skills, so you will be able to talk to others with ease. Sometimes debate partners become friends for life. Even competing debaters from other schools can become your friends.

Making the Most of Your Training

Debate can be one of the best educational experiences in your life. It can help you with your English language skills. It can be exciting and fun. It can also teach you skills that will last a lifetime. Here are a few recommendations to help you make the most of your training:

1. Read your assignments before coming to class. This book and any additional assigned materials will give you background before the session. If you read and understand the material, the class will make more sense to you. Many students take notes on each chapter before coming to class. Writing notes in an organized way is called *outlining*. Outlining is a great way to get the information from the page to your brain.

2. Take notes in class. Many cultures have the same saying: "In one ear and out the other." Perhaps your parents said this to you. It means that when we hear without trying to understand, we will not remember the information. You do not have to record every word you hear in class, but you should write down the main ideas the teacher presents along with your thoughts on these ideas. You will find your note-taking skills improving as you become a better debater.

3. Stay organized. Be sure to organize your notes. Some students type their notes into their computer. Others use a loose leaf binder to organize their notes, outlines from the textbook, and handouts from the instructor.

4. Review the information. Be sure to read your notes as soon after class as possible. Read them aloud and think about what they mean. Feel good about what you are learning. Write down any questions you have for the next lesson. Also try explaining what you learned to someone else. Sometimes teaching a new concept is the best way to learn.

5. Ask questions. As a debater you will learn how to ask questions. If you do not understand a concept, ask your instructor to explain it further.

6. Practice. I teach all of my students the "Five Ps":

   Preparation and Practice Prevent Poor Performance

This text and your instructors and coaches will give you many ideas about how to prepare for a debate. You will also have many opportunities to practice debating in a group or with your partner against another team. You will learn the most in formal practice debates. However, you can always practice alone or with a partner. Practice asking and answering questions, and practice the speeches you have prepared. If you finish a debate and are unhappy with your speech, note where you feel you could have done better so you can avoid those mistakes in future debates.

At the end of every debate, listen to what the judge, your coach, or other debaters have to say. This feedback provides an excellent opportunity to learn what you are doing well and where you need improvement. Take notes on what they say. In the United States, we call these comments *constructive criticism*. The comments are meant to improve your performance, not to make you feel bad about what you just did. Sometimes the judge will write down the comments. Be sure to review these with your coach and teammates so you can improve.

So, you need to read, listen, and speak in order to become a better debater and critical thinker.

Speaking, Listening and Understanding is designed to explain what you need know to get started in debate. It is a beginner's textbook. As you improve, you will want to read other books. I encourage you to continue your education after this course. Perhaps you will learn to love debate as I do, and teach others.

IMPORTANT CONCEPTS IN CHAPTER I

1. People debate for many reasons: to have fun, to take advantage of a great educational opportunity, and to learn effective English language skills.

2. Debate develops a variety of skills, including note taking, organization, research, writing, listening, teamwork, and critical thinking.

3. To improve your chances of success in debate and in school, read assigned materials prior to class, take notes, stay organized, review information learned, ask questions when necessary, and practice.

EXERCISES

1. List the goals you hope to achieve by learning to debate.

2. Get a notebook just for debate. File your notes so that you can refer to them later.

3. Start a vocabulary list. Write down in your notebook every new word you learn.

4. Read. Whether it is newspapers, periodicals, histories, biographies, philosophical works, or even science fiction, nothing develops the mind like reading.

KEY WORDS
brief
constructive criticism
critical listener
oral
outlining
people skills

CHAPTER 2

Debate Basics

This chapter outlines the basics of debating. You will learn who is involved in a debate, the purpose of a debate, and what responsibilities debaters have during a debate.

The first rule of debate:

Two teams agree to disagree about a specific topic.

The Teams

A team may consist of one to four debaters, although most debates have two debaters on each side. A team must either be for the topic or against the topic. When you debate, you can call the other team your *opponent* (regardless of what side you are debating). Depending on the type of the debate, the teams are called different things:

For the topic	Against the topic
Affirmative	Negative
Pro	Con
The Government	The Opposition
Proposition	Opposition

Usually, the teams do not choose what side of the topic they will defend. The tournament assigns the side. Because they do not make that choice, teams do not need to believe in the side of the topic they support. In some debate activities, when the same topic is used for the whole season, the debaters switch sides.

Teams role-play to present the best arguments for their side in a process called *perspective taking.* Like a lawyer who has to defend a guilty client, you may have to defend something that you don't believe. Perspective taking helps you keep an open mind while you search for the best arguments for the side you must defend. Through perspective taking, you also learn how other people think about their side of a topic.

Perspectives on Debate

Many debaters consider debate a game in which the participants sharpen their thinking and speaking skills. Like sports, debate has rules, teams, officials, winners, and losers. Debate becomes mental gymnastics, with teams matching wits against each other. Your job as a debater is to find the best way to achieve victory. Many find the game of debate great fun.

Others debaters think of debate as a laboratory, where one team tests its arguments against the arguments of another. Your job is to do the best job of debating so that the best arguments will emerge. As you improve as a debater, you will become better at testing ideas.

In many cases, students think of debating as a way of finding truth. This means the winning arguments should be the truest arguments.

These perspectives allow debaters to develop the best arguments for a position without injecting their personal beliefs into the debate. To remind everyone that the debate is a contest in which the teams could have been assigned the other side of the issue, the debaters traditionally shake hands at the end of the event. This is a way of indicating that the debate was just a test of skills, not a presentation of deeply held personal beliefs.

The Burdens

A *burden* is a responsibility that each debater is given. Audiences and judges evaluate debaters based on how well they fulfill their burdens. Failure to meet the expectations of the burdens can result in losing the debate. Debaters share three types of burdens:

1. **The Burden of Proof.** The saying debaters use for this burden is, "Those who assert must prove." Whoever wants to make a *point* (an *assertion*) must provide reasons and proof that their point is right. Points, or assertions, are significant, outstanding, or effective ideas, arguments, or suggestions that make up your case. Since most debaters are not experts about the topic they are discussing, they must use sources of evidence that provide valid reasons for the audience to believe the position they are asserting. When a debater asserts a point without

providing evidence, the other side may state the opposite (known as a counterpoint) without evidence, and both sides will tie on that particular point. If neither side gives evidence, the point is not proved and is considered *moot,* or still up for debate.

2. **The Burden of Refutation**. Refutation is the process of attacking and defending arguments. For this type of burden, you could say, "Silence is admission." This means that if you present an argument in a debate and the other team doesn't address it, you win that point automatically, since by its silence the other side has admitted that you are right. The other team is not doing its job, which is to debate your arguments. You win the argument because the other team failed its burden of refutation. When you choose to answer each point or argument the other team presents, you are using line-by-line refutation, because you are following your opponent's organization line by line in your notes and explaining to the judge why each point is wrong (each line in your notes would be another argument). You may also answer several of the other team's arguments with only one or a few responses. This type of refutation is called *grouping,* because you take several lines of argument in your notes and group them together for your answers.

3. **The Burden of Rejoinder**. The saying for this burden is, "Answer the answer." A good debate is like a good table tennis match: when one team hits the ball, the other team returns it. The other team *refutes* what you say. To refute means to prove something the other side said is

wrong. You then have the burden of refuting. You have to prove that the other team's argument or response is weak and your argument is stronger.

The better you handle the three burdens, the better your chances of winning the debate. When the other team has not met its burdens, point this out to the judge. Alerting the judge to the other team's failure should help you win the debate.

The Decision

Debates may have one or more judges. Judges give a win to the team that did the better job in that debate. They are not to consider a team's previous record or vote for the side of the topic that they support.

The judges will write their decision on a ballot and give reasons why they voted the way they did. They will also write individual comments so each debater can improve for the next debate. Sometimes a judge will provide an *oral critique* by specifically telling the debaters what she thought about the debate.

In many debate contests or tournaments, the coaches from one team will judge the debaters from other schools, but they cannot judge their own debaters. This is the only competitive activity in which a coach from one team will give comments to another team on how it can improve. Education is always the number one goal of debate.

IMPORTANT CONCEPTS IN CHAPTER 2

1. Debates take place between two teams, with one to four debaters on each team. One team is for an issue and the other team is against the same issue.

2. There are many ways to perceive debate: as a game or sport, as a laboratory, or as a way of finding truth.

3. Debaters share three burdens: burden of proof, burden of refutation, and burden of rejoinder. Meeting the expectations of the burdens can help a team win a debate.

4. Judges decide who won the debate based on which team did the best job of debating, not on whether they agree with the arguments presented. They indicate their decision on a written ballot and they offer reasons for choosing the winning team.

EXERCISES

1. Write about your favorite food. Write three reasons why you think that food is good. Say your arguments aloud, using three proofs or pieces of evidence.

2. Think of a food that is bad for you. Think of three reasons why people should not eat that food. Say your refutation aloud.

KEY WORDS

assertion

burden

grouping

moot

opponent

oral critique

perspective taking

point

refute

CHAPTER 3

Delivery for Effective Speaking

This chapter teaches you how to best prepare yourself mentally and physically for a debate. Debating can be nerve wracking because you are speaking in public, presenting ideas that your opponent will attack. That's a lot to prepare for! Becoming a more confident speaker will help you in your debating.

When learning to debate, you are also learning how to be a better speaker. As the delivery of your speeches becomes smoother, you will become more confident—not only with your English skills but with your thinking skills as well. This and the next chapter explain the basic concepts that we teach in American public speaking classes. These skills will help you any time you speak in public, including when you are debating.

Fighting Your Fears

Some people have good ideas but are so nervous in their presentation that the audience does not fully listen to them. Others may have weak ideas but "sell" themselves to the audience with great delivery skills. Your goal is to become a genuine and enthusiastic speaker, an honest person who is involved in what you are saying.

First, let's talk about nervousness. Remember, most people have a fear of public speaking. In the United States, we have a term for this type of nervousness: *speech anxiety*. Anxiety is your body's way of preparing you for a dangerous situation. Think about how our ancestors had to protect themselves from wild animals by fighting or running away. In order to survive, they needed a good *fight or flight response*. Your brain thinks public speaking is a dangerous situation, so your body finds a way to increase your strength. When your heart beats faster, more oxygen goes to your arms and legs to make you stronger. You may feel out of breath because you are using up oxygen. You may even move your feet or hands without thinking. All of this comes from your body's extra energy.

Although the fight or flight response is natural, you can control it. Remember, "Preparation and Practice Prevent Poor Performance." If you prepare your body and your mind, you can reduce your nervousness by taking control of the "dangerous situation." Once you have done something several times, your body will no longer think of the situation as dangerous. Even so, some nervousness is a good thing and will help your performance and learning.

Preparing Your Body and Mind for Public Speaking

Here are a few tips that will help you relieve your anxiety about public speaking and debating. To minimize your nervousness, you must prepare both your body and mind.

Preparing Your Body

Eat the right foods. Don't eat large meals or have a lot of meat or dairy products before a debate or presentation. Try to limit eating to bread products, salads, and fruit.

Be sure to drink lots of water. Drink water before your debate and have water with you during the debate in case your mouth becomes dry.

Get plenty of sleep the night before. You may need eight or nine hours of sleep to get your brain and body ready.

Get off your feet. At debate tournaments, you may find yourself standing up between rounds to talk with other debaters. Sit down when talking to conserve your energy.

Practice deep breathing. If you start to have some speech anxiety, go some place quiet, close your eyes, think of a pleasant place, and do a minute or two of slow deep breathing—in through your nose, out through your mouth. Sometimes just a few deep breaths can help.

Preparing Your Mind

Have the right attitude. As a student of communication, you should have this attitude: "I can do this. I am a smart person. I am learning a new skill and this is exciting." Millions of others have learned to debate, and so can you.

Use positive mental attitude or prayer. You may want to use positive statements that focus your thoughts on good performance. Say and think the things you want to have happen. Avoid negative thoughts. If you believe in a higher power, you can use that strength as well. Pray for the help you want. Whatever your beliefs are, do something that helps your mind stay calm.

Act confident so you will become confident. We have a saying in the United States: "Fake it until you make it!" This means that you should never let the nervousness win. No matter how you feel, act as if nothing bad is happening. Follow the ideas on how to be a good speaker and you will become a good speaker.

Give no disclaimers. A *disclaimer* is when you deny responsibility for something. Some people may use a disclaimer before they speak (e.g., "I am very nervous, so this won't be very good"). This only prepares the audience for a bad performance. Usually, the audience will never know if you are nervous or if you have said or done something wrong unless you tell them. Winston Churchill once said, "If you don't tell people that you are sick, they probably won't know." Do not say negative things about your performance before, after, or during the debate.

Focus on your message. You have spent many hours preparing your speeches. You have something important to say. Say it clearly, with confidence.

Concentrate on the audience. The audience came to hear your message. Let them hear it. Remember that they are the reason you are speaking.

Practice

Although preparing your body and mind is very important, practice is the key to reducing your speech anxiety and winning the debate. You may even begin to think of the debates at the tournaments as just one more practice to make you more confident. So, how should you practice?

Practice out loud. Don't just think about your speeches—say them. As you hear the words, you will understand where you need to clarify your arguments or present them in a more exciting way. As you say the words, you will learn which phrases or arguments make the most impact.

Practice with your notes. Use the actual notes you will take into the presentation or competition. Practicing with your notes will ensure that they are adequate.

Practice many times. The more you practice, the better your presentation will be.

Practice in front of an audience. Practice in front of your family, friends, coaches, or other debaters, if possible. If you can't find an audience, practice in front of the mirror.

Practice using all of the delivery techniques. You will read about standing and speaking, gesturing, and eye contact below. Follow all of the delivery guidelines during your practices.

Practice after the tournament. Often during a tournament, you will lose an argument that you shouldn't have lost, because of the way you explained it. When you get home, study your notes and think of ways you could have improved your speech. Also review the judge's comments. Debate judges will give you constructive criticism or positive ways to improve. Your coach, too, may suggest ways of improving. Consolidate their comments and then rework your presentation.

Practice by using new words to make your point stronger. Using well-developed vocabulary that is not overly technical or difficult and that better describes the point you are making will improve your presentation.

Delivery

Now that you understand how to control your nervousness, you need to learn the elements of good delivery to make your speeches sound better and make you look better delivering them.

Be yourself. You don't have to become an actor. Instead, speak as if you are having a conversation. Be your confident self. And remember to be genuine and enthusiastic.

Use vocal variety. Sometimes, the way you say a word brings out its true meaning. You don't want to speak in a *monotone*—everything sounding the same. Instead, allow your thoughts and emotions to come to life by the way you say your words. So, use your tone of voice and speed of delivery to help bring out your meaning. When you speak, stress the important words by using a loud voice, a pause, or saying the word slowly. Speaking in this way keeps the audience interested. Be sure to pronounce your words properly and clearly. Perhaps, you will have to slow down so that everyone can understand you.

Speak up. Make sure that everyone in the room can hear you. Because many non–native-English speakers are not sure of the words they say, they whisper or mumble them to cover any possible mistakes. As a debater, you must learn to project your voice to the back of the room. Projecting is a good way to show confidence.

Control your body. When you have so much energy flowing through your body, your nervousness may come out in negative ways that can hurt your delivery. The best way to get control of your body is to practice using a relaxed position to deliver your speeches. Remember the following:

- Plant your feet. Good speakers do not aimlessly walk around the room or nervously move their legs or feet as they speak. Also, don't move your knees when speaking. Balance your weight on both feet.

- Relax your arms at your sides. Move your fingers or your arms only when you want to gesture. If you have a lectern, you may rest your hands on the top but don't grab or lean on it. The lectern is a great place to put your notes so your hands will be free to gesture occasionally.

- Gestures are acceptable. Don't move your hands constantly. Doing so is called *talking with your hands*.

Instead, move your hands only to emphasize a point. Keep your hands in front of you and above your waist.

- Have eye contact with the audience. Look different audience members in the eyes. Tell a member of the audience a complete thought before going to the next member. Vary your eye contact so that the audience doesn't know where you are going to look next. Be sure that you look at everyone in the audience throughout the debate. Always look at the audience, even when the other team is asking you questions.

- Don't play with your notes. If you have a lectern or desk, place your notes on it. Try not to gesture with your notes, because it will distract the audience from what you are saying.

Use the microphone effectively. If you will be using a microphone, be sure to practice with it in advance. Make sure it is in its proper place and don't touch it. Always leave at least six inches between you and the microphone.

Finally, be conscious of the clothes you will wear during the debate. Although the world is becoming more informal, you should match your clothing to what the audience expects. Sometimes a casual look is appropriate. Other times the event requires more formal attire. In most cases, the audience expects business attire, so you should have clothes for competition that are better than what you would wear to school. Your shoes should be comfortable but polished. Make sure that whatever you wear is neat and clean. If you have long hair, pull it back so it doesn't get in your way.

Avoid dangling jewelry that might distract the audience from your message.

IMPORTANT CONCEPTS IN CHAPTER 3

1. Developing confidence in speaking greatly improves your debating skills.

2. Necessary public speaking skills include fighting your fear, preparing your body and mind, practicing, and speaking more effectively.

EXERCISES

1. Find a short story in a book or magazine. Read it out loud so that the words come to life. Stand up and read the story using appropriate gestures. Assume that you have an audience so that you can practice eye contact.

2. Find a newspaper article and read the words out loud for effectiveness. Put the paper down and summarize the article using vocal variety and gestures.

KEY WORDS

disclaimer   speech anxiety
fight or flight response   talking with your hands
monotone

CHAPTER 4

Organization for Public Speaking

Good organization means presenting your ideas in a way that enables the audience to follow your arguments easily. This chapter teaches you the components of a good speech and describes how to organize and draft speeches that are clear and easy to follow. Debates involve many arguments. If the judges do not know where your ideas fit into the debate, they may not give you a point that you have won. Therefore, you must let everyone know where you are in your presentation.

The Linear Model of Organization

This chapter discusses the *linear* model of organization. Linear means to present something in a straight line. A linear way of organizing means that you present one idea after another so that the audience can follow the line of ideas you are using to prove your arguments. Many U.S. students use the linear model in public speaking or when they write papers. Their teachers can then assess how well the students have proved their points.

The linear model of organization will also help you when you are asked to speak with only a limited amount of time to prepare. This model allows you to organize your thoughts quickly, so you will sound professional when you speak. If you are not using the linear model, you might want to try it when you write your next paper or give a speech. It really helps. The model is organized into six sections:
1. Introduction
2. Thesis statement
3. Preview
4. Body
5. Summary
6. Conclusion

1. Introduction

The goal of the introduction is to get the attention of the audience and set the stage for the topic you will be discussing. You need to gain attention at the beginning of your speech because members of the audience may still be talking to each other. You want them to stop what they are doing and listen to you. You want to peak their interest, but you shouldn't begin with very important information because they may not yet be listening closely.

Good introductions give you confidence and help you win the acceptance of the audience. The first part of the speech is where most speakers are nervous. Knowing that you have prepared and practiced a good introduction will help you relax. And you will establish *credibility* with the audience.

They will assume that you know what you are talking about and will see you as a good source of information.

You can introduce your presentation by using stories, *statistics*, a direct quote, or a joke.

- **Stories.** I recommend this type of introduction because it is the easiest and most effective. Telling a story that introduces your topic draws the audience in easily. Practice your story so you do not have to read it. This way, you will begin your speech with good eye contact. Remember the key points of delivery. Your vocal variety will improve each time you practice the story.

- **Statistics.** Sometimes you can begin your presentation with an important statistic that supports your case, for example, the percentage of people affected by your topic. A powerful statistic helps your audience understand the importance of your subject. Remember to tell the audience the source of the statistic; doing so increases your credibility.

- **A direct quote.** You can begin your presentation with a quote from a highly respected expert on your issue. Sometimes a quotation or saying from a historical figure or a philosopher makes a good introduction. You may even use literature, for example, a poem, to start your speech.

- **A joke.** Some speakers like to start their speeches with humor. Telling a joke increases the audience's interest and makes you likeable. Make sure that the joke fits and that you can tell it in a way that people will laugh. An unfunny, bad, or inappropriate joke may cause the audience to reject your message from the start.

2. Thesis Statement

Once you have finished your introduction, you need a *thesis statement* to tell the audience what your speech is about. Using only one sentence, you should let the audience know the topic and purpose of your speech. Although speeches can cover many different topics, they usually have only three purposes: to inform, to persuade, and to entertain.

- **Speech to inform.** Whenever you want to educate your audience about a subject, you are making a speech to inform. You may demonstrate how something works or how something is made. You may give a report on a specific subject. Your thesis statement for this type of speech could be the following: "Today, I am here to inform you about. . . ."

- **Speech to persuade.** Whenever you want the audience to change what its thinking or to take some action, you are making a speech to persuade. Usually, you identify some problem that needs to be solved and then tell the audience how you intend to reduce or solve the problem. Your thesis statement for this type of speech could be the following: "Today, I am here to tell you what we must do to take care of the problem of. . . ."

- **Speech to entertain.** Whenever you are involved in a speech in which you are not informing or persuading, you are usually entertaining. Sometimes this could be an after-dinner speech that makes people laugh. Perhaps you are trying to inspire at a graduation ceremony. You could also be giving a speech that will help set the tone of a meeting. Your thesis statement for this type of speech could be the following: "Today, we celebrate. . . ."

Remember that your thesis statement should be only one sentence. Make it simple so that the audience will remember it. You will have plenty of time to prove your point.

3. Preview

Once you have told the audience the purpose of your speech, you must tell them how the speech will meet that purpose. You can do this with a preview of the main points you will make. Group your ideas into three-to-five main points so that the audience can better remember your speech. You can even *signpost* your speech by providing numbers for your main points. Signposting means that you provide the order of the arguments you will present. So a speaker previewing a persuasive speech might say: "First, I will talk about the problem. Second, I will discuss the causes of the problem. Third, I will tell you about the solutions to take care of this problem."

4. Body

The body is the most important part of your speech. This is what the audience came to hear. It is where you provide all of the arguments that prove your thesis. The body should be 90 percent of the total speech. When you organize your ideas, you use a pattern that enables the audience to easily follow the progress of your arguments. Using the linear model will help you do this.

Before writing your speech, read all your evidence and separate it into logical groups. Even if you do not have evidence, you may have come up with ideas about your topic. For example, if you were going to talk about your family meals, you wouldn't find evidence in the newspaper, but you would have many ideas about what you wanted to discuss. When you list as many ideas on a topic as you can think of, it is called *brainstorming*. For some speeches you will use brainstorming as a step to guide your research.

Once you have generated all of the ideas that you think you may use, select the best and organize them. You may organize them as you think appropriate, but there are several simple types of organization you can use:

- **Time.** You can explain how things happen chronologically. For example, if you want to demonstrate how to do something, you would show the first step in the process, then the next, and so on. If your presentation includes many steps, group them in three-to-five main points. For example, if you were giving a speech on how to prepare your favorite food, you could have three main points: gather and prepare the ingredients, cook the food, and serve the food. The individual steps would be organized under the main points.

- **Space.** You can organize your main points based on how things are located in physical space or geography. For example, you may analyze the characteristics of students in your classroom by dividing the class in half and first describing the half on your right and then the half on your left. If you wanted to look at trade with China, you might come up with three points: trade with the United States, trade with the European Union, and trade with Japan.

- **Topics.** One of the types of organization is by topic, because every major topic has many subtopics associated with it. Choose the subtopics that best prove your thesis statement. If you are giving a speech on an apple, you may divide the speech into subtopics such as taste, color, and cost. If you are describing how your school is organized, you could discuss the math department, the English department, and the speech department. If you are talking about pollution, you might discuss water pollution, solid waste, and air pollution.

- **Problem-Cause-Solution.** This is a good pattern for a persuasive speech. Your first main point would prove that there is a problem (harm) that must be solved. You would also show who and how many are harmed. This is called *significance* because you are showing how important the harm is to those affected by it. Your second point would prove what causes the problem, and your third how to solve the problem. You would also offer personal action steps that the audience could take to solve the problem or protect themselves from the harm.

Of course, you will find there are many other ways to write a speech or paper. Be creative, but be consistent.

5. Summary
Once you deliver the body of your speech, you should summarize the main points for the audience. Remind the

audience of your thesis statement and preview, but be sure to use the past tense. "Today, we have learned about [your topic]. First, I spoke about the problem, then the cause, and finally the solution."

Repeating your main points will help your audience to remember them. Using the linear organization, you have presented the points in the preview, elaborated on them in the body, and restated them in the summary. You can think about it this way: "I tell them what I am going to tell them, then I tell them, then I tell them what I told them."

6. Conclusion

At the end of the speech, let the audience know your speech is over. Be sure to conclude your remarks with confidence. You may need to take questions or be seated.

Most speakers do not write their speech by starting with the first word and then continuing all the way through to the last word. Instead, they organize and write the body first so that the introduction fits the body and preview mirrors the main points they will discuss.

Organization is central to good debating and public speaking. Good organization will give you more confidence. You will feel more relaxed and have less speech anxiety. The audience will understand your points better, and consequently you will have a better chance of meeting the goal of your speech. And the more you practice organization, the easier it is for your brain to think in organized ways.

Sample Outline

Below is an illustration (without evidence citations) of an outline of a persuasive speech using the problem-cause-solution organization. Note, it is not a complete speech but a narrative outline that a speaker could refer to while giving a speech on the threat of global warming.

1. **Introduction.** Tell the story of the movie *Water World*, in which Kevin Costner stars as the hero who must live in a world after the polar ice caps have melted and Earth is almost completely covered with water. Although the movie is science fiction, it paints a picture of what could happen if we don't do something about global warming. Because the greenhouse effect traps heat, the world will be faced with many new environmental disasters. Yet, if we take strong and decisive actions, we may be able to save our planet for our children.

2. **Thesis Statement.** Today, I urge you to help stop global warming.

3. **Preview.** First, I will describe the increasing problems we can expect from rising temperatures. Second, I'll explore the many causes for this threat. Finally, I will examine what we can do to slow down the damage to our world.

4. **Body.**

I. The worldwide problems of global warming will increase in significance.
A. As temperatures rise, much harm will occur.

1. Farmland will become deserts as temperatures increase. This will lead to food shortages and mass starvation.
2. As oceans water levels rise, saltwater will back up into rivers and destroy freshwater supplies. The lack of water will cause great problems.
   a. 1.2 billion people currently do not have access to clean water. That number will increase with global warming, causing more deaths.
   b. Currently, 2 billion people do not have adequate sanitation, causing many people to become ill. The number of ill people will increase.
   c. Children are most likely to be the victims of inadequate clean water supplies.
3. As farmland and freshwater decrease, more conflicts over resources will cause war.
4. Entire countries and islands will disappear under rising seawater levels, affecting over 100 million people.

B. Changes in climate zones will increase insect-borne diseases.

II. This problem has many causes.
A. Increased use of fossil fuels is the main cause of global warming.
   1. Use of inefficient transportation modes like private automobiles adds to the problem.
   2. Most electricity comes from burning fossil fuels.

B. International treaties are not working.
  1. The United States has not signed the Kyoto Accords.
  2. The European Union ignores the Kyoto Accords.
  3. Developing countries do not have to follow the Kyoto Accords.
  4. The World Trade Organization encourages growth policies that do not reduce global warming.

III. All of us have to act to reduce global warming.
  A. Society needs to take action.
    1. We need to expand green technology in transportation and energy.
    2. Conservation of fossil fuels requires worldwide policies.
    3. The nations of the world need to create ways to penalize nations that hasten global warming, and work together to research ways to reverse the damage.
  B. Individuals need to take action.
    1. Conservation begins at home for all of us.
      a. Take public transportation.
      b. Buy energy efficient appliances/autos.
      c. Shut off lights and appliances when not in use.
    2. Activism is for everyone.
      a. Join environmental protection groups.
      b. Start conservation/recycling in your community/campus.
      c. Speak up for the environment.

5. **Summary.** Today we have learned that the future of life on Earth is uncertain. We now know that global warming will destroy the lives of many and change the way we all live. We have learned that fossil fuel usage and lack of strong government actions is increasing the problem. Finally, we must commit our societies and ourselves to action to reduce global warming before it is too late.

6. **Conclusion.** Thank you for your attention to this important matter. If we can all take action now, perhaps our children will not have to live with a water world in the future.

IMPORTANT CONCEPTS IN CHAPTER 4

1. Using the linear model helps you organize your thoughts quickly and thoroughly.

2. The linear model of organization involves an introduction, a thesis statement, a preview, a body, a summary, and a conclusion.

3. The introduction may consist of a story, statistics, direct quotes, or a joke to get the interest and attention of your audience.

4. The thesis statement tells the audience what you will speak about and whether your speech will inform, persuade, or entertain.

5. The preview tells the audience how your speech will inform, persuade, or entertain.

6. The body is the biggest part of your speech—about 90 percent. It contains all the arguments that support your thesis organized in an established pattern.

7. The summary reminds the audience of the order and components of the speech up to this point and begins to wrap up the speech.

8. The conclusion signals the end of the speech.

EXERCISES

1. Find a quotation from a famous person. Think about three examples that prove that the quotation is true. Write them down. Then think of an introduction (perhaps a story) for the quotation. Give a speech using the linear organizational model. Be sure to use the delivery ideas in Chapter 3. You can give many speeches like this by yourself or you can deliver speeches to other students or your teacher for practice and improvement. This type of speech is called *impromptu speaking*.

2. Find an article in a magazine or newspaper. Using the linear model of organization explain three main points of the article. See if you can find different articles to support these points. Give a speech on the topic, using the articles to explain the ideas.

3. Write a speech that includes evidence you have researched. You might choose a topic such as global warming and the Kyoto Accords.

KEY WORDS
brainstorming
credibility
impromptu speaking
linear
significance
signpost
statistics
thesis statement

CHAPTER 5

Debate Formats

To ensure that everyone has a fair chance to speak, debates have specific rules about speaking order and time limits for each speech. These rules vary depending on the debate format. This chapter discusses the general format of a debate and presents an overview of six popular debate formats.

One of the great things about debate is that everyone is assured an equal opportunity to speak. During your speaking time, you can express your ideas about the topic and what the other team has said about the topic. In arguments that you have outside of debate, this may not be true. Some people may speak more than you or interrupt you. Some may get angry and raise their voices or even threaten you! However, this should never happen in debate. Debate allows for a fair exchange in which all the debaters know how much time they have and when they will speak. It is governed by rules that everyone agrees to follow. The arrangement of the rules is called a debate format.

There are many different formats (number of participants and time limits) of debate in the United States. Most consist of one or two debaters on each side. However, debates in many other parts of the world require three or four debaters per side. In some classroom debates, the teacher may decide to experiment with new rules to fit time schedules or to allow everyone to participate. For example, when I train new debaters, their first debates will usually consist of one-minute speeches, and in their second debates, they have two-minute speeches.

Regardless of the format, the rules should allow everyone equal opportunity to participate. All debaters and judges should be aware of all rules.

General Debate Format

In debates there are two sides: (1.) the *affirmative* team, which supports (affirms) the resolution and (2.) the *negative* team, which rejects (negates) the resolution. The affirmative team usually begins the debate because it may be arguing for a change. Because this is more difficult to do than defending present policy, the affirmative team gets the advantage of speaking first. Also, the affirmative must go first so that the negative knows what to speak against. Most debate formats also allow the affirmative to have the last speech in the debate since it has the responsibility of proposing a change, although this isn't always the case, as you will read later in this chapter.

To be sure that the debate is fair, both teams have an equal amount of speaking time, although the amount of time changes from format to format. If you want to reduce speaking times in the format you create, you must make sure that you reduce times equally for both teams.

In the United States, the judge usually keeps time for the speeches or will ask for a volunteer from the audience. If you are keeping time, be sure to use a good stopwatch and give clear time signals with your fingers. Hand signals are as follows: hold up four fingers when the speaker has four minutes left; hold up three fingers for three minutes; hold up two fingers for two minutes; and hold up one finger for one minute. When 30 seconds remain, you can hold up your thumb and fingers in the shape of a big "C."

In some types of debate, a judge may give oral time signals by announcing how much time is left (e.g., "Three minutes"). When the time is up, she allows the alarm on the stopwatch to sound for all to hear. If there is no alarm, or if the alarm is not loud enough, she should hold up a fist and say, "TIME!" When the time is up, the speaker can finish the last sentence, but to ensure fairness to the other team, judges usually will not listen to arguments given after a debater's time has finished.

In the United States, teams also time themselves. This way, the debater can keep track of the time even if the time-keeper misses a signal. You will need a good stopwatch that counts the time down and has a beep to tell you when time is up. You may also want to use your stopwatch in practices to get used to timing yourself.

Six Popular Debate Formats

The remainder of this chapter discusses the six most popular debate formats. They are Policy Debate, Lincoln–Douglas Debate, Parliamentary Debate—NPDA, Parliamentary Debate—Worlds Style or European/British Parliament, Public Forum, and Karl Popper Debate.

Policy Debate (Cross-Examination)

Policy Debate has existed in the United States for over 100 years. It has several other names: Team Research Debate, Cross-Examination Debate Association (CEDA), National Debate Tournament (NDT), and Oregonian. Typically, policy debaters have the same topic for the entire school year and regularly read evidence word for word during the debate to support their arguments. The wording of the topic is in the form of a policy such as this: "There should be a change in the way Organization X does Y."

Policy Debate calls for two teams: the affirmative and the negative. The first four speeches are each nine minutes long, and each is called a *constructive speech*. During these speeches, debaters may propose or advance new arguments. After each constructive speech, the other team is allowed to cross-examine for no longer than three minutes. The affirmative gives the first constructive speech, followed by a cross-examination from the negative team. The negative gives the second constructive speech, followed by a cross-examination from the affirmative team. The affirmative is allowed to speak again for the third constructive speech, after which it is again cross-examined by the negative. Finally, the negative gives the fourth and final constructive speech, after which the affirmative cross-examines the negative. The teams use all four of their constructive speeches to propose their arguments and inform the audience about their evidence and reasoning to support their arguments.

The last four speeches of the debate are called rebuttals. During a *rebuttal speech*, the debaters are not allowed to present new arguments, since these speeches are meant to challenge the arguments the other team introduced in its constructive speeches. Debaters also use rebuttal speeches to defend their team's arguments from challenges by the other team. Each rebuttal is six minutes long. The negative gives the first rebuttal speech. The affirmative gives the second. The negative is allowed to speak again for the third, and the affirmative gives the fourth and final rebuttal speeches.

The speaking order and time limits are as follows:

Constructive speeches:

First Affirmative Constructive (1AC*)	9 minutes
Cross-Examination (of 1AC by 2NC**)	3 minutes
First Negative Constructive (1NC)	9 minutes
Cross-Examination (of 1NC by 1AC)	3 minutes
Second Affirmative Constructive (2AC)	9 minutes
Cross-Examination (of 2AC by 1NC)	3 minutes
Second Negative Constructive (2NC)	9 minutes
Cross-Examination (of 2NC by 2AC)	3 minutes

---

* AC=Affirmative Constructive
**NC=Negative Constructive

Rebuttal speeches (no cross-examination):

First Negative Rebuttal (1NR*)	6 minutes
First Affirmative Rebuttal (1AR**)	6 minutes
Second Negative Rebuttal (2NR)	6 minutes
Second Affirmative Rebuttal (2AR)	6 minutes

Preparation Time: Because the debates are complex and require significant evidence, each team is allowed a total of ten minutes to prepare for its speeches. This means that if a team takes two minutes "prep time" before its first speech, the team would have eight minutes remaining for preparation before their other speeches.

Lincoln–Douglas Debate

This format uses two people: one for the affirmative and the other for the negative. Lincoln–Douglas Debates can use the same topic throughout the year, but this is not always the case. College debates use a policy topic, while high schools debate a value topic (such as whether or not globalization is more harmful than good). (The different types of topics will be explained in Chapter 6.) The main differences between Lincoln–Douglas and team debate is that there are fewer speeches and you won't be able to depend on a partner to help you.

Notice that even though the same kinds of speech are not the same length for each team, both teams have the same total speaking time.

---

* NR=Negative Rebuttal

**AR=Affirmative Rebuttal

The speaking order and time limits are as follows:

First Affirmative Speech	8 minutes
Cross-Examination	3 minutes
First Negative Speech	12 minutes
Cross-Examination	3 minutes
Second Affirmative Speech	6 minutes
Second Negative Speech	6 minutes
Third Affirmative Speech	4 minutes

Preparation Time: Each debater is allowed six minutes preparation time for the entire debate.

Parliamentary Debate (National Parliamentary Debate Association—NPDA)

Parliamentary Debate—NPDA requires a different topic, also called a motion, for every round. The assembly participant introduces it just like a member would in a national parliament. You might debate motions such as this: "The United Nations should take more action to reduce water pollution."

Tournaments usually have six rounds. In each round, the tournament host will assign teams to debate on the *government* (proposition) or *opposition* side of a new topic. This format has a short preparation time before the debate begins. Once the topic is announced, the teams have 15 minutes preparation time before the opening speech is delivered.

In debate competitions, each two-person team will debate three times on the government side and three times on the opposition side. Note that not every tournament is run the same way. Sometimes the judge in each debate will read the topic in the room and allow teams 15 minutes to prepare. Other times, a tournament official announces the topic to all of the teams in the tournament at the same time, so that each school may prepare as a group and even receive some coaching.

The team affirming the resolution is called the government (gov), or the propositional (prop) team, while the team negating is called the opposition (opp).

The first four speeches are constructive speeches during which the debaters may present new arguments. The first propositional speaker is called the *prime minister* (PM). The first oppositional speaker is called the *leader of the opposition* (LO). The next speaker is the *member of the government* (MG). Finally, the *member of the opposition* (MO) speaks.

The last two speeches are rebuttal speeches, during which the debaters can present no new arguments. The LO has the first rebuttal speech, and the PM finishes the debate. There are no cross-examination periods in parliamentary debate, but the other team may ask for a *point of information* of the speaker during the constructive speeches. The other team uses points of information to ask a question to clarify or make a point. You do this by standing up during an opponent's constructive speech and ask, "Point of information?" The speaker does not have to take the question and may say, "Not at this time." To take a question, the speaker says, "Yes, what is your point?" The participants cannot ask questions during the rebuttal speeches or during the first minute or last minute of each constructive speech.

Because no new arguments are allowed in the rebuttals, the other team may interrupt the speaker with a *point of order* to ask the judge to determine if the speaker is presenting a new argument. To do so, a debater stands and says, "Point of order." The judge then says, "*State your point.*" Then the debater must explain why she thinks the argument is new. The judge may decide it is not new and allow the argument to stay in the round. The judge would then say, "*Point not well taken.*" If the judge agrees that it is a new argument and he will not consider the argument in the debate, he will say, "*Point well taken.*" The judge may also say, "Taken under consideration," and decide later if the argument was new or not.

The speaking order and time limits are as follows:

Announce topic and pre-speech preparation time 15 minutes

Constructive Speeches:

Prime Minister Constructive (PMC)	7 minutes
Leader of the Opposition Constructive (LOC)	8 minutes
Member of the Government Constructive (MGC)	8 minutes
Member of the Opposition Constructive (MOC)	8 minutes

Rebuttal Speeches:

Leader of the Opposition Rebuttal (LOR)	4 minutes

Prime Minister Rebuttal (PMR)   5 minutes

Preparation time: There is no additional preparation time between speeches. The only preparation time is the 15 minutes given before the debate begins.

NPDA Parliamentary Debate is different from other formats in several ways:

1. There is no preparation time between speeches. Debaters are expected to rise to speak as soon as the other team has finished.

2. Debaters have titles within the debate as described above and belong to teams that have names different from simply affirmative and negative.

3. There is no cross-examination period in parliamentary debate.

Parliamentary Debate (Worlds Style or European/ British Parliament)

In *Parliamentary Debate—Worlds Style or European/British Parliament*, four teams compete at the same time with two two-person teams on the propositional side and two two-person teams on the oppositional side. All speeches are seven minutes long. The four teams prepare their arguments separately and all compete against each other. The judge will decide which teams did the better debating based on the strength of their arguments and the style of their delivery. The top team in the debate would be awarded three points, the second best team receives two points, the third best team gets one point, and the fourth team gets no points. In some cases, one of the teams representing the proposition could be awarded three points, while the other receives none.

In the Worlds style debate, speakers may still accept or reject a point of information as in the NPDA style, but this format does not allow points of order.

The speaking order and time limits are as follows:

Announce topic and pre-speech preparation time	15 minutes
First Opening Propositional	7 minutes
First Opening Oppositional	7 minutes
Second Opening Propositional	7 minutes
Second Opening Oppositional	7 minutes
First Closing Propositional	7 minutes
First Closing Oppositional	7 minutes
Second Closing Propositional	7 minutes
Second Closing Oppositional	7 minutes

Public Forum

Public Forum (also called *Ted Turner Debate* or *Controversy*) is one of the newest events in U.S. high school competition. Public Forum attempts to get more students involved by making the event an audience-oriented contest, usually without expert debate judges involved. This event is similar to what audiences have come to expect from news programs like CNN's "Crossfire." New topics, chosen for their balance of evaluative arguments on both sides, are announced each month on www.nflonline.org. Debaters use evidence but usually will not read it verbatim during the debate. The two-person teams in Public Forum are *pro* (affirmative) and *con* (negative). The resolution can either be a policy or a value topic.

Before the debate, the teams flip a coin, with the winner choosing either to be pro or con or to be the first or last speaker. Unlike the other formats, the con may begin the debate. The team that speaks first will not speak last.

Instead of cross-examination speeches, Public Forum has *crossfire*. During this time, the debaters who just finished speaking can ask and answer questions of each other.

The summary speeches allow the debaters to recap the best arguments for their side. This is a chance for more refutation but not new arguments. In the *last shot*, each team will reprise the ONE argument that they believe will win the debate for them.

The speaking order and time limits are as follows:

Team A Speaker 1	4 minutes
Team B Speaker 1	4 minutes
Crossfire (between A1 & B1)	3 minutes
Team A Speaker 2	4 minutes
Team B Speaker 2	4 minutes
Crossfire (between A2 & B2)	3 minutes
A1 Summary	2 minutes
B1 Summary	2 minutes
Grand Crossfire (all speakers)	3 minutes

| A2 Last Shot | 1 minute |
| B2 Last Shot | 1 minute |

Preparation Time: Each team is allowed a total of two minutes of preparation time between speeches.

Karl Popper Debate

The Karl Popper debate format calls for two teams: affirmative and negative. Each team has three debaters, with each debater speaking once in the debate. The same topic can be debated for the whole year or the topics can be new for each tournament.

The speaking order and time limits are as follows:

Affirmative Constructive	6 minutes
First Negative Cross-Examination	3 minutes
Negative Constructive	6 minutes
First Affirmative Cross-Examination	3 minutes
First Affirmative Rebuttal	5 minutes
Second Negative Cross-Examination	3 minutes
First Negative Rebuttal	5 minutes
Second Affirmative Cross-Examination	3 minutes
Second Affirmative Rebuttal	5 minutes
Second Negative Rebuttal	5 minutes

Preparation Time: Each team is allowed a total of eight minutes of preparation between speeches.

Karl Popper Debate permits more students to be involved because there are three students on a team. It also requires

students to speak only once, so novices find it an easier way
to start their debating career.

Conclusion

The different formats were designed to make each debate as
fair as possible. Like any sport, debate has rules that allow
the competitors to prepare and that give all the competitors
an equal chance to win. You can easily follow the formats
I have explained or create your own. Remember, fairness is
the number one goal when setting up a debate.

IMPORTANT CONCEPTS IN CHAPTER 5

1. Debate formats are Policy Debate, Lincoln–Douglas
   Debate, Parliamentary Debate, Public Forum, and Karl
   Popper Debate.

2. All formats have an affirmative and a negative team,
   both of which have the same amount of total speaking
   time.

3. Policy Debate involves teams debating a current policy.
   Typically, debaters have the same topic for the entire
   school year and read evidence word for word during the
   debate.

4. Lincoln–Douglas Debate has only one person on each team, and the topic remains the same throughout the year.

5. There are two types of parliamentary debate: National Parliamentary Debate Association and Worlds Style or European/British Parliament. Both involve the two teams taking the roles of governmental leaders. This format requires a different topic for every round.

6. Public Forum introduces new topics each month and does not permit the use of expert debate judges.

7. Karl Popper Debate permits more people to be involved because there are three students on a team.

EXERCISES

1. Conduct a debate in your class using a fun topic on something dealing with your school. Organize the class into groups of four to six so that two students are the pro team, two students are the con team, and one to two students are judges. You may want to reduce the time limits for the debate. Perhaps each debater speaks for only one or two minutes. Make sure one of the judges in each group serves as the timekeeper.

2. Take notes on a debate and explain which team won and why.

KEY WORDS

affirmative

con

constructive speech

Controversy

crossfire

government

Karl Popper Debate

last shot

leader of the opposition

Lincoln–Douglas Debate

member of the government

member of the opposition

negative

opposition

Parliamentary Debate—NPDA

Parliamentary Debate—Worlds Style or European/British Parliament

point of information

point of order

point not well taken

point well taken

Policy Debate

prime minister

pro

Public Forum

rebuttal speech

state your point

Ted Turner Debate

CHAPTER 6

Propositions

The two sides in a debate must have a specific *topic* to argue. This topic is worded in the form of a *proposition*—a statement to be proved. This chapter presents an overview of the three main types of propositions and teaches you how to develop an effective proposition.

Developing a Proposition

The proposition (also called the topic, *resolution*, or *motion*) should be very clear so that both sides know what they are to argue. When developing a proposition, you must consider the following:

1. The proposition must involve a debatable topic, one on which people can disagree. For example, you couldn't debate a topic like "Humans need oxygen to live," since there is no alternative to this proposition for the negative to advance.

2. The proposition should entail only one statement for the affirmative to prove. Proving two things (a *complex statement*) is difficult. For example, the proposition

"Information should be free and available to everyone" requires the affirmative to prove (a.) that information should be free and (b.) that information should be available to everyone. Because there are multiple factors involved, the affirmative would have difficulty proving it.

3. The proposition should have enough arguments on both sides so that the debate is fair. When this type of fairness exists, both sides are said to have *fair ground* in the debate.

4. The topic must hold the interest of the debaters over the course of the debate period. Some national debate associations in the United States use the same topic for an entire year. Those associations spend many months researching the topic to be sure that the topic area will allow both sides to have arguments over the course of many tournaments.

Propositions fall into three categories: propositions of fact, propositions of value, and propositions of policy.

Propositions of Fact

A *proposition of fact* is a statement that can be proved using some kind of a measurement. When we can prove something using a statement based on an observable event or measurable facts, we say that the statement is an *objective statement*. If you were to say that someone is two meters tall, you could objectively measure that person to see if the statement is correct. When we make a statement and then use some agreed measurement to prove the truth of that statement, we are using *objective verification*. If the statement and the measurement match (if the person is two meters tall), then the proposition of fact is *valid*. If we make a statement and the measurement proves us wrong (if the person is 1.5 meters tall), then the proposition of fact is *invalid*.

Of course, a debate involves far more important topics than a person's height. It could be about environmental damage and may involve the number of people who have been harmed by air pollution. If you were debating this topic, you may find a scientific report that claims to prove how many people suffer because of bad air. So, you could use statistics or a statement by an expert to prove a proposition. Your opponent would then try to prove that your measurement or statement was incorrect or that better evidence proves you wrong.

Propositions of Value

A *proposition of value* requires the affirmative to persuade the judges and audience to accept an opinion or value. You debate values all the time. You argue with your friends about whether a certain movie is good or not. You have opinions about what food is best. You may even argue about which of your teachers is best. There is no right or wrong to a *subjective opinion* since it is simply what someone believes, not what someone knows. When you argue a proposition of value, you are trying to provide evidence that your subjective opinion is better than the other team's.

Arguing a proposition of value involves more steps than just making a statement and backing it up with a measurement as we saw in propositions of fact. Here's how you prove a value:

1. Provide a general definition of the value term you are discussing. Let's keep this simple. A proposition of value may be the following:

   It is too cold in our classroom.

   The value term "cold" is not a fact; it is an opinion, since some people feel cold when others feel hot. However, when you give the general definition of cold as "being a low temperature," you are letting everyone know that you will not be discussing a specific temperature, which is a fact that can be measured.

2. Provide the specific definition for the value term. This is called the *contextual definition* for the value. In other words, you are telling the audience what "too cold" means for the *context* of the classroom. The contextual definition would be different if we were talking about the temperatures for a food freezer, which should be very cold. In this case, the contextual definition of "cold" is the temperature at which students cannot learn because they are too cold to focus on the lesson. Since students are in class to learn, you could ask about the value: "What temperature allows students to learn the best?" This contextual definition would provide the highest value for the specific term.

3. Provide standards of measurement, or *criteria*. Use criteria to show that you have justified your value in asking, "What is the best temperature for learning?" You could find these criteria from a variety of sources. You might find a study evaluating classroom temperatures, or perhaps your teacher might know the *appropriate* (suitable) temperature. Based on such sources, let's say you can show that the best temperature for learning is 21° C.

4. Now that you have provided a definition of "cold" (a low temperature), the context of the value term (the temperature below which students cannot learn because they are too cold to focus on the lesson), and the criteria (the best temperature for learning is 21° C), you must provide proof that supports the criteria. Since you now have a proposition of fact (less than 21° C is too cold for students to learn in a classroom), you measure the temperature. If it is less than 21° C, you have justified your value that the classroom is too cold for learning to take place. If it is higher than 21° C, you did not justify the proposition based on the definitions, context, and criteria you provided.

As you can see, in order to confirm values, you must provide facts. In effect, you can change a proposition of value into a proposition of fact. You can take a value term like "cold" and turn it into an objective verification like "the temperature in the classroom is less than 21° C."

The example we've used is simple. However, debating values will often be more difficult because it involves issues more important to you than temperature. You may debate the morality of specific actions. For example, you may debate whether watching television is good or bad for children. Or you may weigh the relative benefits of two things: for example, economic prosperity vs. environmental protection. If you are defending the proposition as part of the affirmative team, you must provide definition, context, criteria, and proof. Your opponents can attack any or all of these. They may say that your definition is wrong or your context is not appropriate, or perhaps there are better criteria for judgments. Or, as when debating a proposition of fact, your opponent can even prove that your measurement is wrong or that you don't have the best facts.

Proposition of Policy

A *proposition of policy* recommends taking a certain action. If you can justify a value and that value is based on facts, you are recommending that value as well as ways to promote the value. For example, you have found research showing that arts education improves students' critical thinking skills and you want your school to offer more arts classes. Based on this research, you could debate that having the school change its class offerings would be better for students, or would reduce a harm such as poor student preparation for college, or would come closer to a value such as better test scores. You do not have to prove that your school will change. The question for the affirmative team in a policy debate is this: If an action were taken, would the results be desirable?

In order to prove the desirability of a proposition of policy, the affirmative has to prove what are known as *stock issues*. These are *harm, significance, inherency*, plan, *advantage*, and *solvency*:

1. You must prove that there is a need to change the current policy because the situation is harmful. Your harm could be the people who die or are injured, have psychological pain, lose their quality of life, are subjected to a lower standard of living, or lose their independence because of the current state or situation.

2. You must prove that there is a significant need. In some cases, you might want to show how many people are affected by the current policy. If you are discussing an environmental problem, for example, you might describe how it impacts humans or discuss how it seriously affects an ecological system. Or perhaps you would prove that some value, such as a culture, is being lost by current actions or policy.

3. You must prove inherency. Inherency means that the *status quo* (Latin for "current system") is not solving the problem. Perhaps social attitudes or bad laws are causing the harm. Whatever the inherency, you need to show how it exists and that it allows the harm to continue.

4. You must provide a plan to solve the problem. A plan is the action you would take to reduce or eliminate the harms the status quo is causing. You need to include

several points in your plan. You need to explain who will take the action (*agent of action*); what will be done (*mandate*); how you would pay for the plan (*financing*); and who will make sure the plan is carried out (*enforcement*). The individual points of the plan are called *planks*:

- Plank One: Agent of Action. An agent of action is the individual, group, or government that will adopt the plan.

- Plank Two: Mandate. A mandate is the specific action the plan requires.

- Plank Three: Financing or Funding. Financing lists specific sources of *funding*, such as taxes.

- Plank Four: Enforcement. Enforcement indicates the specific agency that will implement the mandates.

5. You should prove solvency or how the plan will solve or reduce the harm you presented in stock issue one.

6. You should provide advantages or additional benefits to the plan. These advantages may not address the harm directly but will discuss other good things that will result from adopting the plan, thus provide more reasons to accept the proposition.

You can present these stock issues in many different ways. Regardless of how you present them, you must remember that when proving a policy proposition, you must provide the policy you want to put into effect (the plan) and explain why it would be good (the case). So, in order to prove a proposition of policy, you must also have facts and values on your side to make your case.

Your opponent may argue against your case or any or all parts of your plan to prove that you have no need or an insignificant need, or that the status quo is solving the problem. The opponent might also show that your plan won't work or that it will cause more harms than the status quo. An attack that shows that adopting your plan is worse than the status quo is called a *disadvantage*. It is each team's job to show that their side has more significance than the other side.

Propositions guide the debate so that the debaters know what they must prove. They also provide fairness before the debate so the debaters know their ground. Propositions allow debaters to research and think about their arguments in order to have well-informed debates.

IMPORTANT CONCEPTS IN CHAPTER 6

1. There are three types of propositions: fact, value, and policy.

2. Propositions of fact are statements proved with some kind of measurement. Objective verification proves these propositions to be valid.

3. Propositions of value are value or opinion statements that the affirmative attempts to prove by giving a general definition of the value term, a contextual definition for

the value term, criteria of the value, and proof that supports the criteria.

4. Propositions of policy are recommendations that a certain action be taken to change a current policy or situation. To prove the desirability of the recommendation, the debater must prove stock issues: a significant need for change, inherency, solvency of the harms, and advantages. The debater must also provide a detailed plan that includes the agent of action, mandates, funding, and enforcement.

EXERCISES

1. List five topic areas. Write three propositions for each topic (one fact, one value, and one policy).

2. Listen to a discussion on TV. Are the people debating facts, values, or policies?

KEY WORDS

advantage	disadvantage
agent of action	enforcement
appropriate	fair ground
complex statement	financing
context	funding
contextual definition	harm
criteria	inherency

(continued)

invalid

mandate

motion

objective statement

objective verification

planks

proposition

proposition of fact

proposition of policy

proposition of value

resolution

significance

solvency

status quo

stock issues

subjective opinion

topic

valid

CHAPTER 7

Case Development

In the previous chapter you learned about three kinds of propositions. This chapter provides detail on how to develop your arguments to support your proposition. In debate, your job is to present the best ideas you can to support the side you represent. To do this, you must organize your best arguments and present them clearly to other participants, the judge, and the audience. This is called developing a case. A case is one or more arguments sufficient to support a proposition. How you develop a case depends on whether you are the affirmative or negative and what type of proposition you are debating.

Affirmative Case Development

When the affirmative meets all of the expectations of the burdens associated with the type of resolution (fact, value, or policy), it is said that the affirmative case is *prima facie*, Latin for "on its face," or literally "first face." This means that the affirmative has met enough of its burden of proof to support the proposition. If the affirmative team does not meet the burden throughout the course of the debate and therefore does not provide a prima facie case, it should lose the debate.

You may be creative in presenting your case, but when judges get used to a specific type of organization, they tend to reward those teams who meet their expectations. While this book is not a comprehensive guide for all aspects of debating, judges generally adhere to the basic standards presented here. You should try to match what the judges are looking for with the type of organization you use. Since the majority of topics deal with policy propositions, we will first look at their organization.

Policy Propositions

A case for a policy proposition might have the following organization:

I. Resolutional Analysis

    This is an observation that provides the framework for the affirmative's case. It may include one or more of the items listed below. Let everyone know the position you are taking on the resolution. Then provide the following:

    A. Definition of key terms. You do not have to define every word, only those that are important for the debate. To be fair to the other team, your definitions must be reasonable. Some teams will even provide the source of their definitions.

    B. Resolution type. Tell the judge which words in the resolution allow you to argue that this is a policy resolution. You would analyze the verb that makes the resolution a call to action.

C. Burdens. Explain what you must prove to win the debate.

D. Decision rule. Indicate to the judge that your team won the debate because your plan has more benefits than the other team's plan.

II. Needs

This is the part of the affirmative case that identifies a certain problem that the existing system cannot solve. When presenting the need, you must discuss the following:

A. Harms. Explain what bad things are happening under the existing system. You may also want to point out how a value is involved. For instance, you could discuss how a group of people is being treated unfairly because of the current situation.

B. Significance. Describe the importance of the harm. There are two different types of significance, quantitative and qualitative. *Quantitative significance* provides numbers (X number of people are being hurt); while *qualitative significance* provides why the value is important (why protecting Y is important). You may decide to prove both or only one type of significance.

III. Inherency

This is the cause of the problem, the attitude or law that allows a condition/harm to exist. Describe either or both of these types of inherency.

A. Attitudinal Inherency. Explain what attitudes or feelings are causing the problem. Examples are greed, ignorance, apathy, and prejudice.
B. Structural Inherency. What policies or laws could be improved to limit or stop the harm?

IV. Plan
This is a course of action the affirmative proposes to solve the problems identified in the need. To show how you propose to stop or reduce the harm, you must discuss the following:
A. Agent of action. Explain who will take the action.
B. Mandate. Describe what must be done to stop or reduce the harm.
C. Funding. Indicate who will pay for the plan.
D. Enforcement. Specify who will enforce the plan.

V. Solvency
Solvency explains how the plan will stop or reduce the harm by providing analysis and evidence in support of the plan.

VI. Advantages
This section demonstrates the positive effects of the plan, the good things that will come from it.

Value Propositions

With a value resolution, the affirmative does not have to present a plan but rather just provide evidence to support the claim made by the resolution. The outline below illustrates how to construct a case for a simple value proposition.

I. Resolutional Analysis
    This is an observation that provides the framework for the case. It may include one or more of the following items. Let everyone know the position you are taking on the resolution. Then provide the following:
    A. Definition of key terms, including a general definition of the value term.
    B. Resolution type and appropriate context. This states whether you are making a value judgment or comparison. This is where the contextual definition would present the *highest value*.
    C. Criteria. This is a measurement that determines when enough evidence has been presented to prove a position.

II. Examples or Proof
    A. You must provide examples or proof that support your criteria. Include as many specific points (*observations* or *contentions*) as you have time for.

Fact Propositions

Developing a case for a fact proposition is similar to developing one for a value proposition. The *resolutional analysis* for the fact proposition is similar but the case for a fact proposition has a special focus on the criteria. Since a proposition of fact needs to objectively prove a statement, the affirmative must present an acceptable measurement in the criteria. Then the affirmative must provide a point at which we know that they have proved the criteria, and thus proved their argument. This is called a *threshold*. Once the resolutional analysis is given, the team must present contentions, specific points to prove the proposition valid.

Negative Case Development

The negative can win a debate through effectively arguing against (refuting) the affirmative case. But to increase their chances of victory, the negative must present a planned and careful case to supplement its response to the affirmative's. This independent argument, or case, is called a *counter-case*. If you choose to use a counter-case, you would craft an argument in the same way that the affirmative crafted its. You would organize your thoughts with your own specific points (*counter-contentions* or *counter-observations*). You should label them "Counter-Contention One," etc. before stating them. Remember that these arguments are not a direct refutation of the affirmative case but are independent reasons for rejecting the affirmative and the resolution.

IMPORTANT CONCEPTS IN CHAPTER 7

1. How you develop a case depends on the type of debate proposition: policy, value, or fact.

2. A policy debate involves resolutional analysis, details about needs, inherency, a plan, solvency, and advantages.

3. Case development for value and fact propositions does not involve a plan but does include resolutional analysis and examples or proof.

4. Developing a negative case may involve creating a counter-case with counter-observations to reject the affirmative's resolution.

EXERCISES

1. Write a case for a policy topic. Make it something fun. Resolved: All students should be taught to dance.

2. Write a case for a value topic. Resolved: Art is more important than science.

KEY WORDS

contentions
counter-case
counter-contentions or
   counter-observations
highest value
observations

prima facie
quantitative significance
qualitative significance
resolutional analysis
threshold

CHAPTER 8

Critical Thinking

ritical thinking is thinking about how you think. It
is the process of asking and answering questions and
trying to understand how and why you come to the conclusions that you do. This is an essential skill for debate
because debaters need to plan what they will say, antici-
pate the other team's response, and think of an argument
to counter the other team's arguments. Debate is not just a
discussion between two sides. Rather, it is a contest in which
each side is trying to win by presenting a better argument
and making the other team's argument look less reasonable
or weak.

This chapter describes the main parts of an argument
and shows how critical thinking is necessary to create the
strongest, most cohesive argument possible. The chapter
also describes how to recognize flawed arguments and use
your opponent's flaws to your advantage.

Critical thinking is not just something we should strive
to use in debate; it should be part of everything we do. You
can use many skills to become a better critical thinker:

1. Comparing the viewpoints of other people to your own way of thinking or your perspective;

2. Finding ways to ask questions that apply to many perspectives;

3. Understanding why some statements are correct and others are not, while still understanding the uncertainty of knowledge;

4. Researching through critical reading and evaluation;

5. Understanding how problem solving works;

6. Establishing criteria for making judgments;

7. Presenting arguments in a constructive way.

Many other skills are involved in developing critical thinking. When you learn to argue and defend your own position, you are a critical thinker. When you argue against another's position, you are a critical thinker. When you change your mind because of the arguments you hear, you are a critical thinker. When you understand that argumentation occurs whenever someone communicates to influence others to change their beliefs or behavior, you are a critical thinker.

Constructing an Argument

Arguments in debate must be well thought-out and have a line of reasoning that is relatively easy to follow. Therefore, you must use critical thinking when constructing an argument. *Argument construction* occurs when you are making an argument for or against a certain viewpoint. Do not confuse this with <u>having</u> an argument with your friends over the best movie of all time.

According to Stephen Toulmin, a British philosopher, an argument is something made to support a position. It may be as simple as a single statement or it may be a chain of arguments used to answer a complex question. To understand an argument, we can use the *Toulmin Model*. This model divides an argument into three main parts called a *triad*.

1. **Claim.** Whenever you make a statement that you want others to accept, you are providing a *claim*. There are three types of claims: fact, value, and policy.

2. **Grounds.** When you make statements that provide facts to support the claim, you are giving the *grounds* for your claim. We usually call this *evidence*, but it also can be called proof, research, data, support, documentation, or substantiation.

3. **Warrant.** When you make statements to show how the facts are connected to the claim or provide the reasoning for your arguments, you are providing the *warrant*. This is also called *analysis*.

Here is an example of the three parts of an argument in a Toulmin Model:

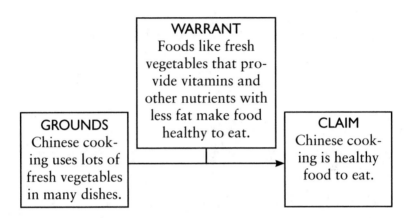

As a novice debater, you might find the Toulmin Model a bit difficult to understand, but you should learn how to use it because it helps keep your argument linear and to the point. Many times, you will not actually need to say the warrant or analysis, but it must be implied in your arguments. Analysis that is not spoken is called an *implied warrant*. You can still have a complete argument if your warrant is implied. However, if you have not stated a warrant, the other team can attack your argument more easily.

Analyzing Arguments

In very basic terms, an argument must prove a claim. Whenever an argument does not, it is called a *fallacy*. One of the most difficult skills you must learn in debating is recognizing fallacies. You need to use critical thinking to avoid them in your arguments and to alert the judge when your opponent uses them.

Although debaters can use improper reasoning in many ways, fallacies usually occur in one of the three areas of an argument: claim, grounds, or warrant. See how each of the fallacies below violates the rules associated with the Toulmin Model. The list below includes only a few types of fallacies.

Fallacies Involving Claims

Equivocation. Debaters make an *equivocation* when they use a word in two different senses and the meaning of the word is shifted during the argument. For example, let's say a debater argues that all men are created equal, but that Nancy is a woman, therefore she cannot be equal. In this case the use of the word men refers to people in a general sense of humans as a species, not specifically the male gender. Therefore, this is a shift in the meaning of the word "men."

Amphiboly. This fallacy arises when the grammar of a sentence makes it ambiguous. Here is an example of an *amphiboly*: if a debater says that the government will give $100 million to Chad and Congo, does this mean each country will get $100 million or that they will have to divide the money in some way?

Fallacies Involving Grounds

Begging the Question. Whenever an argument makes a claim and then provides evidence that is the same as the claim, it is *begging the question*. The following is an example. A says, "Gary is telling the truth." B says, "Why do you say that?" A replies, "Because he wouldn't lie to me."

Circular definition (tautology). To give a *circular definition (tautology)* is to define a term by using the same term. "A bad law is a law that is bad" is an example.

Question begging epithets. When an adjective or adverb is added to a term to form an additional argument, it is a *question begging epithet*. For example, to call someone a cowardly pacifist is to say that not only is the person against war, but is against war because of fear. In this case te term is making two arguments. Someone who is a pacifist may have a great deal of courage to hold that position, so we cannot assume that a pacifist is also a coward just because someone put the adjective "cowardly" in front of the noun "pacifist."

Straw argument (also straw man or straw person). Intentionally misinterpreting an opponent's argument and then defeating it is committing a straw person fallacy. For example, if Team A says air pollution is bad, and Team B argues that Team A is wrong because water pollution isn't that bad, Team B is creating a *straw argument* or *straw man*.

Red herring. To divert attention from the main argument to something insignificant is called using a *red herring*. For example, if the argument is about bad drinking water and the other team asks questions about how swimming pools are filled, they are using a red herring.

Ad hominem attack. To attack the debater and not the argument is an *ad hominem attack*. Debaters also commit this fallacy when they attack someone for the group he belongs to. For example, if someone says "he doesn't know what he is talking about because he is too old," she has used an ad hominem attack.

Appeal to the people. To say that something is true because the majority of people support it is an *appeal to the people*. Popularity doesn't necessarily make something true. For example, saying that millions of people like to eat fast food, so it must be good for them is an appeal to the people.

Appeal to authority. When a debater says someone's opinion is final and that there can be no argument with it, he is making an *appeal to authority*. For example, if I say my expert is the most respected in her field, and so, no one can defeat her position, I am appealing to authority.

Hasty generalization. When we jump to conclusions by using too few examples or examples that are not typical of the group, we are using hasty generalizations. For example, if you meet two Americans who do not like hot dogs and you say that all Americans don't like hot dogs, you are giving a *hasty generalization*.

Accident. The opposite of a hasty generalization is when we think that something that is generally true applies to an entire group. For example, if you know that Americans love to drive cars and you conclude that John loves to drive a car, because he is from the United States, you have committed an *accident*. John may only ride a bicycle because it is good for the environment, and he may not like to drive.

Fallacies Involving Warrants or Unwarranted Assumptions

Non Sequitur. This is Latin for "does not follow." The term describes an argument in which the claim or conclusion does not follow from the reasoning or grounds provided. For example, Bill eats McDonald's hamburgers; therefore he supports globalization. This is a *non sequitur*.

False cause. There are many types of *false cause* fallacies. Two of the most common are post hoc fallacies and correlations.

1. **Post hoc.** This is Latin for "after the fact." Sometimes people will claim that because something came first, it caused something that came after it. This is called a *post hoc fallacy*. Here's an example: "Gary is from California, where it is sunny. Since he came to visit our school, there have only been sunny days. Therefore, he must have caused the good weather."

2. **Correlation.** In looking at two things that don't cause each other but are related to a third thing that causes both of them, we have a fallacy of *correlation*. For example, when someone says, "Increased ice cream sales causes increased murder." We know that ice cream doesn't cause murder but both increased ice cream sales and increased murder are a response to higher temperatures.

False analogy. Using a comparison, like a simile, may be a good literary device, but it is a weak argument and a *false analogy*. <u>All analogies are false analogies.</u> For example, "I hate this argument like a cat hates water" provides no grounds or warrants to support a claim.

Your job as a debater is to present the best arguments you can construct. At the same time you need to attack the arguments of the other side. As you get better at critical thinking, you will start to recognize faulty reasoning in others. Sometimes the fallacies will fit into neat little groups like the ones I listed above. Other times they will be complex. Regardless, you need to develop the ability to explain what is wrong with the thinking of others. And when they analyze your thinking, you need to defend your arguments and explain that you have good reasoning.

Cross-Examination

Cross-examination is a short period of time at the end of constructive speeches given to one team to ask questions of the other team. <u>The purpose of the cross-examination is not to argue with the other team but to gather information to support your case.</u> Critical thinking is key at this point because debaters must determine where they are going with their arguments in light of what the other team has said. The cross-examination period is the time when one team has the chance to question the other to highlight deficiencies in the opponent's case and build up support for its case. So you must think carefully—and strategically—about both your questions and answers.

When you are asking questions of the other team

1. Face the audience when speaking. Do not face your opponent. Stand next to the speaker and slightly behind him or her.

2. Ask simple questions that require "yes" or "no" answers as much as possible.

3. Do not allow the person to answer with a long, involved explanation.

4. Be polite when interrupting your opponent if her answers are too long.

5. Do not allow your opponent to ask you questions. Politely remind them, "This is my cross-examination period."

6. Do not make arguments during cross-examination.

7. Use your opponent's answers from the cross-examination during your next speech.

When you are answering questions from the other team

1. Face the audience.

2. If you need to explain your answer, tell your opponent you cannot answer "yes or no" and need to qualify your answer.

3. Do not try to ask questions unless it is to clarify a question.

4. When the time is finished, you do not need to answer any more questions.

5. Think before you speak.

Points of information

Many types of debate permit a debater to interrupt the speaker and ask a simple clarifying question—if the speaker allows it. Points of information keep the speaker on task and allow the opposing team to point out inconsistencies in his argument. Thinking critically is vital when requesting points of information. Teams must use these strategically to point out flaws in the other teams' arguments while highlighting their own plan. Determining which questions will help your team, how to word the questions, and when to ask them involves a keen game plan. Randomly requesting points of information only serves to annoy the judges and audience and may hinder your case. But thinking and planning about how and when to ask the right questions are good debating techniques.

Asking points of information

1. Stand and wait to be recognized before interrupting the speaker.

2. If the speaker does not see you standing or allows you to stand unrecognized for more than five seconds, politely ask, "Point of information?"

3. Look at the audience when asking your questions.

4. Ask your question in less than 15 seconds and sit down after asking your question.

5. Do not ask questions during the first or last minute of the constructive speeches.

6. If the speaker does not want any more questions, do not interrupt the speech.

7. Be sure to ask at least one good question to prove to the judge that you know what is important.

Answering points of information

1. Look at the audience.

2. When your opponent stands for a point of information, either take the question or ask her to sit down. Do not leave her standing without some recognition.

3. When accepting a question say, "Your question, please?"

4. When not accepting a question say, "Not at this time."

5. Take at least a few point-of-information questions. If you do not take questions, the judge will think you are not being fair to the other team. The number of questions you should take is not fixed, but many in the United States think three is a reasonable number.

6. Provide good answers to the questions. If the question is about something you will discuss later, tell the questioner to be patient and that you will get to it. You do not have to answer the questions, but the judge may take that into consideration in coming to her decision.

When you ask and answer questions, you are trying to make the best impression you can on the judge. You want to appear fair, polite, and intelligent. You want to use each question as a way to get the judge to like you more.

IMPORTANT CONCEPTS IN CHAPTER 8

1. Critical thinking is central to arguing a position and attacking an opponent's position effectively.

2. Using the Toulmin Model enables a debater to make a sound argument that flows from grounds to claim.

3. A fallacy is an unsound argument and typically occurs in one of three areas of argument: claims, grounds, and warrants.

4. During cross-examination and by the strategic use of points of information, a team can strengthen its arguments and weaken its opponent's.

EXERCISES

1. Look for advertisements in magazines and newspapers. See if you can spot any fallacies.

2. Look at the cases you wrote for the last chapter. Write down some questions you must answer to help prove your point.

3. Think of some questions that the other team might ask you. Practice the answers you would give.

KEY WORDS

accident

ad hominem attack

amphiboly

analysis

appeal to authority

appeal to the people

argument construction

begging the question

circular definition

claim

correlation

critical thinking

cross-examination

equivocation

evidence

fallacy

false analogy

false cause

hasty generalization

grounds

implied warrant

non sequitur

post hoc fallacy

question begging epithet

red herring

straw argument

straw man

tautology

Toulmin Model

triad

warrant

CHAPTER 9

Research

In Chapter 2 you learned that if you make an assertion, you must prove it. You must provide evidence. This chapter explains how to gather evidence and organize it so that you can find it quickly during your debate.

The Importance of Evidence

You now know that you must give grounds (offer proof) to complete an argument. You also know that if a debater makes an argument without proof, the opposing team can challenge it. When two non-experts (as debaters usually are) make an argument against each other without proof, neither side wins the argument. That argument is considered *moot*, which means it is still uncertain who will win the argument.

To prove an argument, you need facts and information that support it. The only way to get these facts is through research. In some debates, you have little formal preparation time, and so you must constantly be alert for information you think might be useful. By watching the world news regularly, reading newspapers, and researching especially important topics, you will build up a wealth of knowledge to use at your next debate. These topics might include taxation, criminal and civil justice, political systems and philosophies, privacy and individual rights, social justice, labor and economic policy, international affairs and policy, media, pop culture, education policy, health care, and family matters.

Researching

Some of the best lessons you can learn from debating will come while researching. You will learn where to find good sources of information and how to evaluate evidence. You will be able to defend your research and attack that of others. Most significantly, you will learn the importance of using your research honestly. You want to have a reputation for being a thorough and honest researcher.

When researching, you should focus on both sides of an issue. You could be assigned either side of an argument, and if you collect evidence or information to support only the side that you agree with, you will be at a loss if you must argue the other side. Remember, too, that debate is not about defending your personal viewpoint but about defending the position assigned and convincing the judges and audience that you actually support it. You must also research both sides of an issue because you have to be prepared for the arguments the other team presents.

What to Look for in Your Research

Evidence is any piece of information that helps a side prove its claim. There are various kinds of evidence you can use to support your case. Three of the most important are the following:

Statistics. Whenever you need to prove significance, you should use data, if possible. You should find out how many people are affected by the issue or what percentage that number means in comparison to the whole. For example, the World Bank states that 1.2 billion people in the world do not have access to clean water. This means that of the 6.425 billion people in the world, 18.7 percent of the population uses polluted water.

Examples. Another way of showing significance is by using an example. For instance, to illustrate the dangers of global warming, you may say: "My example is Tuvalu, where 80 percent of the island is seven feet or less above sea level. If the trends continue, the island will disappear in the next century due to rising sea levels caused by global warming." You could also use an example to show how your plan will succeed by presenting a case in which it has worked in the past or a similar plan that is now working.

Testimonials or Expert Opinions. Sometimes experts can provide an opinion that supports your position. This is called a *testimonial*. For example, based on research, scientists working for the United Nations in their millennium ecosystem assessment (www.millenniumassessment.org) indicated that destruction of ocean fisheries posed the greatest threat of starvation on the planet. You could use this fact to support a case about denying oil drilling rights in coastal areas because the resulting destruction of healthy coastal ecosystems harms or kills fish. An expert may offer suggestions on how to solve a problem or provide you with a philosophical basis for a value that you could use.

Finding the Evidence

You can find evidence in several ways. As you now know, you can uncover evidence everyday by reading newspapers and magazines, but you can also find evidence on the Internet and in the library. Both sources have pluses and minuses.

The Internet

Many people rely on the Internet for a quick, easy way to access all kinds of information. And because sites are updated regularly, you can use the Internet to find the most current information on your topic. Remember, though, that there is so much information available it is easy to become overwhelmed; so construct your search terms carefully. A good starting point for your research is Debatabase, sponsored by the International Debate Education Association. It can be found at http://www.debatabase.org.

When using the Internet, you must evaluate the information you find very carefully, because many sites are not reliable and do not go through the extensive editorial and review process that many print sources do. To evaluate a site, ask yourself the following questions:

- Who are the authors of the site?
- What are their qualifications?
- Might they have a bias? Is the site associated with groups that advocate a specific position?
- What date was the information put on the Web? When was it last updated?

The Library

Today, many researchers don't go beyond the Internet. This is a mistake. You need to use the library for background and history as well as in-depth analysis of your topic. Books, specialized magazines, scholarly journals, dissertations, etc. can help you delve deeply into your topic, and because these sources go through an extensive editorial process, the information is likely to be accurate.

Many libraries also have access to a wide variety of electronic materials that can be extremely helpful in researching your topic. Some of the most useful resources for debaters include the following:

- Congressional Quarterly Researcher, http://library2.cq-press.com/cqresearcher/
- EBSCO Research, http://support.epnet.com/CustSupport/AboutUs/AboutUs.asp
- EHRAF Collections of Ethnography, http://library2.cq-press.com/cqresearcher/
- Global Books in Print, http://www.globalbooksinprint.com/GlobalBooksInPrint/
- InfoTrac Databases, http://web5.infotrac.galegroup.com/itw/infomark/

- JSTOR journal storage, http://www.jstor.org/demo.shtml
- Lexis-Nexis Databases, http://www.lexis-nexis.com
- Project Muse scholarly journals online, http://muse.jhu.edu/about/contact.html

You must plan your trip to the library just as you plan your Internet search. Write down the topics you wish to research and the key words associated with them so that you can use the library's electronic catalog efficiently. And remember that the library has one big advantage over the Internet: the reference librarian. He or she will be very willing to answer any questions you have, describe the resources available, and help you focus your research. These professionals are invaluable.

Reading and Cutting the Evidence

Once you find the evidence you are looking for, you need to put it into a usable form. Many debaters use a "cut and paste" technique either with their computers or with scissors and tape. When you find some useful information, you cut the information out and transfer it to a fresh piece of paper. You may also use a computer program to cut and paste the information into a file. Put only one piece of information on each sheet so that you can file it for easy reference. At the top of the sheet write a claim that the evidence supports. Also include a source citation for each piece of evidence. List author, qualifications of the author, publication, date, page number, and, if a website, electronic address (URL) and date of access.

Organizing the Evidence

To debate successfully, you must be able to locate your information quickly. Therefore, you must organize it efficiently.

Once you start gathering evidence, you should put all the evidence about one area or topic into a single file so you can see what you have. If the main topic file gets too thick, divide the topic into subtopics and create files for each. The key to filing is to arrange the information so that you can find the evidence quickly. Remember, you will have very little time to find the evidence you need during a tournament. If you can't find it in a few seconds, you need a better organizing system. Read through your evidence regularly so you become familiar with your files and adjust the organization if necessary.

How you organize the information that you gather is important. In some types of debate, like policy debate, you are expected to read your printed evidence. This is called *direct quotation.* In other formats, such as parliamentary debate, you may not read specific quotations from evidence during your speeches. This means that you must be familiar with the research you have read and be able to tell the judge about the proof. Offering the evidence to the judge without reading it word for word is called *paraphrasing.* In fact, debaters in parliamentary debate learn to develop a *narrative.* This means that they will put together a summary about what they may have learned from many sources. Debaters may practice delivering information many times so that they can develop strong explanations. Remember, only the notes you have written down during preparation time can be used during a parliamentary debate.

Building Arguments

Once you have enough evidence, you can build arguments using the information you have. This is called building a *brief*. A brief is a short written version of the argument. Since all debates are timed, you usually cannot read all of the evidence in your file. You must make choices. Take the best evidence and write briefs using it. Remember that while the brief is short, it must have a complete argument with evidence or your opponent can easily attack it.

Testing the Evidence

Not all evidence has the same value. To be valuable, evidence must be *recent, relevant, and reliable.*

Recent. How old is the evidence? Timeliness is not an issue in some areas, such as philosophy or religion. But when dealing with current events, the judge usually will trust the newest evidence. If you have evidence from last week that an international treaty doesn't have much hope of adoption and your opponent has evidence from today that major countries have signed the treaty, your opponent's evidence is better because it is more recent. Situations and laws change, so you must be prepared to defend the currency of your evidence.

Relevant. Does the evidence prove the point? Your evidence must be directly related to the claim it is to support. If it isn't, you actually have offered no evidence. To determine relevancy, ask what kind of methods the author used to reach his or her conclusions.

Reliable. Are the sources trustworthy? Is the source qualified? You want to quote an expert on the topic, someone with advanced training, who has conducted research, or who has experience in the field. When evaluating the reliability of a source, ask yourself the following questions:

- Is the source in a position to know the truth?
- Was the source a witness to the event?
- Does the source have a bias?

Be sure the source is objective. He or she should be unbiased and report what actually happened without allowing emotions or imagination to intrude. Once again, you should be able to defend the type of methods your sources used.

I have judged many debates in which the quality of research determined the winner. You want to be an expert on the issues. Having better research is a powerful tool for defeating your opponent.

IMPORTANT CONCEPTS IN CHAPTER 9

1. Debate requires good research skills to gather evidence that you can use at a moment's notice.

2. Statistics, examples, testimonials, and expert opinions are excellent types of evidence.

3. To evaluate evidence, determine if it is recent, relevant, and reliable.

EXERCISES

1. Read an article by an environmental expert. Be able to state the qualifications of the source. How many individual pieces of information can you find in the article?

2. Find several articles on a topic that interests you. Cut and paste the evidence onto different sheets of paper. Find the evidence that supports one part of your case (e.g., harms).

3. Develop a contention with at least three pieces of evidence that support your argument.

4. Start files of evidence on your topic.

5. Find the three types of evidence (statistics, examples, and expert opinions) in a newspaper article.

KEY WORDS
brief
direct quotation
moot
narrative
paraphrasing
recent, relevant, and reliable
testimonial

CHAPTER 10

Refutation and Rejoinder

This chapter explains one of the most crucial parts of a good debate—*refutation*. Before refutation takes place, the two teams are really just presenting what they want you to know about their side of the issue. Refutation is when you show that your argument is stronger than your opponent's or that your opponent's argument is weaker than yours. Refutation almost always involves countering the evidence that the opposition presented, blurring the link between its evidence and its argument, and/or ripping apart the argument's reasoning. In earlier chapters, you learned how to make your arguments stronger. This chapter shows you how to challenge your opponent's arguments successfully.

Repeat, Refute, Replace

Refutation is a process that involves three steps:

1. **Repeat** the argument you are going to refute. Provide the number your opponent used when he presented the argument. For example, "Go to the first contention on the

harms of the status quo." This *signposting* will help the judge locate the argument.

2. **Refute** the argument. Explain what is wrong with the other team's argument. Look to the claims, grounds, or warrants. You might say, "Their evidence is old; it is from two years ago." If you have many reasons why the argument is flawed, let the judge know how many arguments you have and number each one ("I have four arguments against this point, first . . .").

3. **Replace** the argument with your argument. For example, "My evidence from two weeks ago proves the situation has changed from the time of their evidence."

Make sure that your refutation is organized and that it includes all three steps. Good organization is the key to winning the debate. A debate can be won or lost on one argument. So, be certain that the judge can follow your presentation.

Refutation Techniques

You can use the following techniques to carry out the repeat-refute-replace process effectively.

1. Use signposting in the repeat phase

Signposting is when, at the beginning of the speech, you tell everyone the organization and order of your refutation. This is also called presenting a *roadmap*, because you are telling the judge, your teammate, the other debaters, and the audience the order of your arguments. When you first address the audience, announce which arguments you will speak to first, second, and so on. If you don't let everyone know where you are on the flow sheet, they will miss one or more of your arguments. By telling everyone what argument you are discussing, the debate stays organized.

2. Clash in the refute phase

Clash means that the two teams are directly debating each other's arguments. You want to clash with your opponent's arguments. This is a technique used in the refute phase. When the other team does not clash with your arguments, you need to point that out to the judge. Remember, "Silence is admission." If you don't counter the other team's arguments, you are agreeing with those arguments. If the other team does not clash with one of your arguments, you should win that argument. Unfortunately, beginning debaters often fail to clash, primarily because they are disorganized. If you can stay organized and clash with the other team by directly refuting its arguments, you will likely win the debate.

3. Employ direct refutation in the refute phase

Direct refutation is when you point out the flaws in the opponent's argument. Sometimes you will go straight down your flow sheet in the same organization as the earlier speeches in the debate. When you say something about every point, this is called *line-by-line refutation*. You may have more than one argument against each line of argument by the other team. During the debate you should tell everyone where you are on the flow sheet and what your answer is so they can write it down.

4. Group arguments in the replace phase

Grouping arguments is when you refute multiple arguments of the other team with only one argument of your own. If an entire contention is flawed because it is based on old evidence, you may defeat it with one argument attacking the relevance or reliability of the evidence.

5. Include impact in the replace phase

Impact is why the argument is important. You should always ask yourself, "What does this argument do for my position?" Use your answer to explain the impact to the judge. If the other team does not explain the impact of its argument, you should point that out to the judge. The way you explain the impacts of your arguments and your opponent's arguments will likely make a difference in the decision of the judge.

Constructing Arguments

You can use two types of arguments during refutation: on-case and off-case. When the negative attacks the issues that were defended in the first affirmative speech, it is presenting an *on-case argument*. When the negative offers a new argument that does not directly address those the affirmative has presented but is a significant reason for rejecting the case or plan, it is presenting an *off-case argument*.

Regardless of which type of argument you use, you should consider the following:

1. **Solvency.** When you prove that the plan will not solve the need, you are showing the judge there is no reason to vote for the plan. You can attack the solvency arguments by directly refuting the case or you can prove that the plan is not workable. Perhaps you can prove there are other causes the plan does not address and these causes will continue the harm. For example, if the affirmative wants to stop air pollution by reducing coal burning but encouraging the use of oil, there is no solvency because burning oil also results in air pollution.

2. **Disadvantage.** The most important argument against a plan is a disadvantage. You want to point out the harmful things that will happen because of the affirmative's plan. I tell my debaters they should start with disadvantages against a plan whenever they negate a policy proposition. The disadvantage is a *cause-effect argument*. The plan is the cause and the negative impact of the argument is the effect. For example, if the affirmative plan involves spending money on a new governmental program, that money must be taken from somewhere else. If you can prove that some other important program will be hurt, that would be a disadvantage.

3. **Criteria.** In a value debate, the affirmative team must provide criteria, or *standards* of measurements, that are fair to the opposition. The negative team does not have to accept these, and may provide better counter-criteria. By doing so, the negative indicates that the proposition is not being proved and that it has a better case for rejecting the proposition.

4. **Topicality.** If the affirmative provides definitions or a plan that does not meet the resolution, it is not topical. Unless the affirmative is topical, the negative does not have fair ground to argue against the resolution, and the affirmative deserves to lose. By arguing that the affirmative is not topical, the negative is saying that the judge cannot vote for the affirmative because it is not debating the topic assigned. To argue *topicality*, the negative must address the following:

   a. <u>Definition of term</u>: Tell the judge what *term* or word in the resolution the affirmative defined inappropriately.

   b. <u>Standards</u>: Explain how we should evaluate whether the definition provides fair ground for debate. Remember to examine the source of the definition to determine if the definition is the best or most appropriate available. For example, using a scientific dictionary to define a physics term is better than taking the definition from a general magazine article. When you provide the way you want the judge to view the term, you are providing standards.

   c. <u>Violations</u>: *Violations* occur when the other team has not met the standard. Explain this to the judge. In a policy debate, your focus should be on explaining how the affirmative's plan does not address the assigned topic.

   d. <u>Voting issue</u>: Finally, you must explain to the judge why your argument is a *voting issue*, the reason why you should win this debate on this argument alone.

You can tell the judge that the affirmative presented a case that did not fit the topic assigned. Therefore, it didn't follow the first rule of debate: to agree to disagree on a specific topic. You may also tell the judge that she does not have the authority to decide this debate because it was not on the assigned topic.

You may present several different topicality arguments in a single debate. The affirmative must win the topicality argument or it loses the debate. But even if the affirmative wins the topicality argument, it still has to win its plan and case to win the debate. On the other hand, topicality is a "no-lose argument" for the negative. If the negative wins a topicality argument, it wins the debate; if the negative loses it, the team can still win on other issues. The negative team should not overuse topicality. But it is a good way to make sure an affirmative team is not presenting a case that doesn't debate the topic.

Rejoinder

Remember that both teams have a "burden of rejoinder" (to address the responses of the other team). A good debate is like a table tennis match: both teams keep returning the argument back to the other side. So, when it is your turn to speak, be sure that you give a *rejoinder* to the argument and do not just repeat it. Repeat the main argument and the last argument of the other team; then give your response. If the other team does not answer one of your arguments, tell the judge the argument was dropped and that your team's last argument is now the only argument left. Then stress the impact of the argument ("this is important because . . ."). If an argument has no impact, don't waste time addressing it. Remember, arguments are only valuable if they have some impact on the position of either team.

IMPORTANT CONCEPTS IN CHAPTER 10

1. Refutation is showing the opponent's argument as weaker than yours or showing that your argument is stronger.

2. The basic process of refutation can be summed up as repeat-refute-replace.

3. Techniques used in refuting an argument include signposting, clashing, refuting directly, explaining impact, and grouping.

4. The negative can use on-case arguments or off-case arguments to respond to the affirmative's argument.

5. In refuting the affirmative's argument, the negative should address solvency, disadvantages, criteria, and topicality.

Exercises

1. Read a newspaper editorial. Think of reasons why you might support the editorial and why you might reject it. Give a speech about both sides.

2. Develop a plan for refuting a topic of your choice. Come up with an on-case AND an off-case argument that will respond to the affirmative's argument.

KEY WORDS
cause-effect argument
clash
direct refutation
grouping
impact
line-by-line refutation
off-case argument
on-case argument
refutation
rejoinder
roadmap
signposting
standards
term
topicality
violations
voting issue

CHAPTER 11

Note Taking and Flowing

This chapter explains the importance of debaters and judges taking notes during a debate. Debaters call this process *flowing* a debate. You will learn how to use a *flow sheet* in flowing and will compare a completed flow sheet to the actual debate that it flowed.

Importance of Notes

To win in debate, you need to take good notes. You have to remember the other team's arguments and the order in which they were presented. You also need to jot down your responses so that you can present them in an organized manner. Taking organized notes is important because you must be able to tell the audience exactly where an argument fits in the debate before you state your own points. And if you are ever a judge, you must be able to explain to the debaters what arguments were important and why. Although you may initially find taking notes difficult, most debaters eventually become so good that following their instructors' lectures in classes is easy.

Flowing a Debate

Skilled debaters, audience members, and judges use a flow sheet to follow the progression of arguments in a debate. When you write down the arguments in a debate, you are "flowing the round." You do this by dividing a sheet of paper into columns—one for each speech—and then write your notes on each speech in its own column. With eight speeches in a debate, you would divide the sheet into eight columns. Note that while a flow sheet initially starts with one page, you can use more sheets if you need more space to record your notes.

When the first speaker presents the affirmative case, write down the main points in the first column. Good debaters will number the points they present so that everyone can track the argument during the debate. You should write down the arguments regardless of the team you are on. Both sides need to flow the entire debate.

If you are addressing the other team's argument, tell everyone what argument you are discussing, first by repeating the argument (with its number listed) and then by providing an organized refutation. If you have multiple responses to an argument, make this clear. For example, you would say: "On the first contention I have three arguments. My first argument is. . . ." If you are presenting new arguments in support of your own case, then let the audience know that.

Make sure that you remain organized so that the judge can flow the arguments. Many judges will say a point for a team counts only "if it gets written on the flow." What this means is that if the judge misses your argument because you were disorganized in your speech, you will have lost that point.

When your debates are over, you may want to keep your flow sheets and file them for later discussion with coaches and teammates. Flow sheets are especially helpful when writing a summary of the debate. This summary will help you to prepare if you ever debate the same topic again.

Shorthand

Arguments can come very fast in a debate, so you will not be able to write down every word. Consequently, you need to find ways to *abbreviate* words (also called *shorthand*) to make sure you record all the information you need. You may also use arrows (‡) to show where each argument fits into the debate. If a debate involves many arguments, some debaters use very small handwriting or larger paper or many sheets of paper, with each contention on a separate page. Each page is divided so that each speech has its own column.

You may want to develop your own symbols so you can flow faster. Here are some of my favorite shorthand abbreviations:

agent of action	A of A
because	b/c
better	B
billion	bil
contention	C
cost benefit analysis	CBA
criteria	Crit

decrease	↓
disadvantage	DA
dollars	$
dropped	[D]
enforcement	Enf
evidence	ev
funding	fund
greater than	>
impact	imp
increase	↑
inherency	INH
is/equals	=
less than	<
linear	/
link	L
million	mil
not equal	≠
not	∅
number	#
observation	O, obs
policy	P, pol
quantify	Q
question	?
should not	s/n
should	s/
significance	sig
solvency	sol
status quo	SQ
therefore	∴

thousand	K or M
topicality	T
uniqueness	U
voting issue	VI
with	w/
without	w/o

To see how a flow sheet corresponds to an actual debate, refer to the debate transcript and accompanying flow sheet in the Appendixes.

IMPORTANT CONCEPTS IN CHAPTER 11

1. Good note taking is one of the attributes of good debating.

2. Flow sheets chart a debate and allow the debaters, the audience, and the judges to track arguments.

EXERCISES

1. Practice your flowing skills when you watch or listen to the news. Write down the main points. During the commercial break, give a short speech on what you heard, presenting the main points in an organized manner.

2. Flow every debate you watch. It is great practice.

3. Try to flow a teacher's lecture. Draw a line down the middle of your note paper. Write the teacher's comments on the left side and your comments about the lecture on the right side. You will have to stay focused to do this successfully. Later, try to reconstruct the lecture from memory and see how much more you remember when you review your notes.

KEY WORDS
abbreviate
flow/flowing
flow sheet
shorthand

CHAPTER 12

Tournaments and Judges

This chapter discusses how to put your debating skills to the test by either participating in a debate tournament or observing one. While observing a tournament may not sound like a challenge, you will find that it is an excellent way to practice anticipating arguments, identifying fallacies, and flowing debates. You will come away excited about debate!

Some students may be satisfied with debating in the classroom, but others enjoy *tournaments*, which allow students to compete against debaters from other schools. Tournaments add interest to debating. Every year hundreds of tournaments are held in the United States because competition is a good way to develop and demonstrate knowledge and skills. Teams that want to be champions want to debate against as many good schools as possible. The more experience they have against good teams, the more they will be prepared for the championships.

Tournaments

As a *novice* debater, you will probably not yet be ready to participate in debate tournaments, but it is definitely a good idea to attend them as an observer and watch how practiced debaters organize their arguments and take on their opponents. Without a doubt, this will help you develop your debating skills and prepare to one day take part in a tournament.

Local, state, and national associations hold tournaments. These associations have specific rules for their contests. But any school may decide to hold a tournament and invite other schools. These tournaments are called *invitational tournaments*.

If you are a more seasoned debater ready to take part in a tournament, your coach will help to decide which tournament(s) to take part in. When the coaches at my school decide which tournaments to attend, we look at how much the tournament will cost and what kind of experience our students will have. Tournaments charge fees to cover expenses like awards, meals, and judging. Schools must contact the tournament officials to register, usually three days to three weeks before the tournament begins. Schools must also provide one qualified judge for every two teams or pay an additional fee so that the tournament can hire a judge.

We make sure to attend the California state championships, where all of the community colleges can compete against each other. However, because there are so many national tournaments, we must select the few tournaments we can afford.

The motto of my team is "Education—Ethics—Excellence." My students may attend between 15 and 20 tournaments per school year to get the best education they can, but they also go to win, while all the time being honest and ethical debaters.

Tournaments generally take place on weekends. Sometimes the tournaments are close enough that we can drive to them each day. The van may leave at 6:30 A.M. and come back at 9:00 P.M., meaning students give up their weekends as well as their sleep! Sometimes a tournament is far away, so we have to stay in a hotel. Other times a tournament may be so far away that we have to fly there. Debate competition in the United States can involve a lot of time and a lot of money.

Most U.S. tournaments have six *rounds*, when all the teams compete at the same time. These rounds are called the *preliminary rounds*. There is usually only one judge in each debate room. The tournament will make sure that each team gets to debate an equal number of times on each side—affirmative and negative. So, if there are six preliminary rounds, you should debate three times on the affirmative and three times on the negative. At the end of the preliminary rounds, the administrator of the tournament will add up the wins and losses of every team. The top teams will then debate in the elimination rounds. During these rounds, once a team loses a debate, it is eliminated from the tournament. In deciding which team makes it to the elimination rounds if two teams tie with the same win-loss record in the preliminary rounds, the tournament administrator will look at the total score of each team's individual speaker points. The team with the higher points is judged the better team for the elimination rounds. Special computer programs compute the win-loss records and points for each team and debater.

When all teams have competed and a winning team has been decided from each debate, the finalists from each debate compete in a final round. If the tournament is small, with four to seven teams competing, the tournament may skip the elimination rounds and stage only a final debate between the top two teams. If the tournament is large, with 200 or 300 teams, 64 teams might participate in the elimination rounds.

Scheduling

A typical schedule for a four-round, one-day tournament may look like this:

8:00–8:30 A.M.	Registration
8:30–9:45	Round one
9:45–11:00	Round two
11:00–12:15	Round three
12:15–12:45 P.M.	Lunch
12:45–2:00	Round four
2:30–4:00	Quarter-final elimination round
4:00–5:15	Semi-final elimination round
5:15–6:30	Final round
6:30	Awards ceremony

Divisions

At the beginning of the tournament, teams are separated into three different *divisions* based on experience: novice, *junior*, and *open debater*. Although the rules vary from tournament to tournament, most U.S. tournaments use the following definitions. A novice is someone in his or her first year of competition who has not yet won a tournament or someone who has debated for less than 30 rounds in competition. Novices will compete only against other novices. Juniors are debaters in their first two years of competition who have not yet won a tournament at the junior level. All other debaters are open debaters. Anyone can compete as an open debater, even a novice, but novices generally have a harder time winning in this category.

Teams in all levels receive awards. Each team that advances to the elimination rounds receives a trophy or plaque. The individual debaters who scored the most points during the preliminary rounds also receive speaker awards.

Judges

A judge's primary duty is to determine which team did the better job of debating and to give speaker points to each debater. When making their decisions, judges focus on the quality of each team's arguments and the way in which each team responded to the opponent's arguments. They also judge organization and the important verbal and non-verbal elements you learned about in chapter 3. A typical scale allows for 1–30 points for each debater. A perfect score of 30 points would be very rare; most judges would not give under 20 points, even in a novice round.

Judges are expected to be objective. They are to decide which team wins based on what happened in the round, not on a team's previous record or on their own opinion about the topic. Judges never judge their own teams.

In addition to determining a winner and awarding points, judges have other duties as well. These include keeping time and giving time signals to the teams. They may also have to make decisions in the middle of the debate. In parliamentary debate, for example, if a team brings up a new argument in the rebuttals, the other team may call a point of order and ask the judge to decide if the argument is new or not.

Judges are committed to judge every round. However, at least three judges are assigned to each elimination round debate (although more can be used, as long as it is an odd number so there can't be any ties).

You will have many different judges during your debating experience. Sometimes the judge may be a coach from another school and a debate expert. Other times the judge may be a teacher, who, although intelligent, is not an expert in debate. You may also have students judge you. In the United States, college students are hired to judge high school tournaments. Sometimes these students are debaters and can be experts. Still another judge may never have seen a debate before and is known as a *lay judge*. When a tournament is low on judges, open debaters may judge the novices.

It doesn't matter if you have an expert or a lay judge in your debate. Your job as a debater is to try to win the ballot. Therefore, pay special attention to what the judge says and try to debate to please him or her. This approach is called *adapting*. You must adapt to the judge—the judge does not adapt to you. Before the round begins, judges should explain their judging philosophies and tell you their experience levels. Sometimes judges provide written philosophies that are distributed to all teams before the tournament begins.

Ballots

Ballot information includes the following:

1. Division: novice, junior, or open

2. Round number: preliminary 1 through 6 or elimination round (i.e., semi-finals or finals)

3. Room number

4. Judge name

5. Topic: in parliamentary debate the topic will be different each round

6. Team on the affirmative/government (school and code if given)
   - Name of first speaker
   - Name of second speaker

7. Team on the negative/opposition (school and code if given)
   - Name of the first speaker
   - Name of the second speaker

8. Rank: the best speaker gets 1st, second best gets 2nd, and so forth

9. Rate: points given to each speaker (1–30 points each). Sometimes there are boxes to check with an "x" and other times just total points are required

10. Winner of the debate: side and school name

11. Judge signature and school represented

12. Written comments in the bottom half of the paper about each debater and an explanation of the decision about who won and why

At the end of the round, the judge fills out a ballot and turns it in to the tournament administrator. The format or design of the ballot can be different for different tournaments, but they all have the same vital information. The ballot is duplicated so each team will have its own copy. Here is what the top of a ballot looks like for a parliamentary debate:

PARLIAMENTARY DEBATE

Division _____ Round _____ Room _____ Judge_____

Topic_____

Proposition Team _____ | Opposition Team _____
from_____School | from_____School

Names of debaters	Rate (1–30)	Rank (1–4)	Names of debaters	Rate (1–30)	Rank (1–4)
Leader:			Leader:		
Member:			Member:		

Circle the winning team

Comments and reason for decision

_____

_____ | _____

Judge's signature | Judge's school

Ballot Review

You will receive a copy of the ballot at the end of the tournament to share with your coach and team. You should discuss what the judge wrote and learn how to improve for the next debate based on the judge's comments. In addition to writing comments on the ballot (called a written *critique*), the judge may also provide an oral explanation (an oral critique) of the decision at the end of the debate. This is a time for you to listen and take notes. Do not argue or debate with the judge. Even if you disagree with what the judge is saying, listen and thank her or him for the comments. Afterward, you can share with your coach and teammates the comments that the judge gave you. If you debate before the same judge again, you can use the comments to adapt to her or his style of judging.

Perhaps, one day, you too will become an expert and judge a debate. But before that day, your teacher may call on you to be a judge during informal classroom debates. When you are a judge, you have an obligation to make a fair decision. You must leave personal feelings aside and determine a winner based only on what happened in the debate and who did the better job of debating. You must also be prepared to offer both positive and negative <u>constructive</u> comments to help the teams learn from their debating experience. You should be able to justify your decision based on the arguments you have heard. Remember to flow the entire debate carefully. Many times debaters will stop taking good notes after they have finished their own last speech. But judges must continue flowing until the last word spoken because they do not know what may be important until the debate is over.

Conclusion

Tournament competition is exciting and fun. It is also one of the best educational opportunities in your life. Not only do you learn oral English and critical thinking skills, but you also develop interpersonal communication skills. Perhaps you will be involved in international debates and learn more about intercultural communication. You will learn the importance of teamwork. You will also learn about disappointment and how to handle losses when things do not turn out as you expected. Debate lessons are life lessons. Learning how to accept the wins and losses in debate will help you deal with the joys and disappointments of life.

More practically, debate looks very good on your resume when you apply for college and graduate school or try to get a job. It means that you care about learning, as well as how to think and how to speak better. I hope you have many opportunities to debate and discover the same enjoyment I have found.

IMPORTANT CONCEPTS IN CHAPTER 12

1. Competing in debate tournaments is an excellent way to improve your English skills and become a better debater.

2. Tournaments can have many different formats, but most U.S. tournaments have six rounds involving all teams.

3. The competitive divisions in a debate tournament are novice, junior, and open debater.

4. Judges must be fair in their decisions and also provide critical feedback to debaters.

EXERCISES

1. Participate in as many debates as you possibly can.

2. Enjoy yourself!

KEY WORDS
adapting
critique
divisions
invitational tournaments
junior
lay judge
novice
open debater
preliminary rounds
rounds
tournaments

Appendixes

DEBATE TRANSCRIPT

The following transcript is from a Parliamentary Debate.
The two teams are composed of the following debaters:

Proposition	Opposition
Prime Minister: Dan Neidle	Leader of the Opposition: Rob Weekes
Member of the Government: Seb Isaac	Member of the Opposition: Andy Kidd

The topic was <u>We felt safer during the Cold War.</u>

In Parliamentary Debate, the Government, or Proposition, side is expected to argue that we felt safer during the Cold War. The Opposition is expected to argue that we feel safer now, in the post–Cold War era.

This transcript is verbatim (word for word) and so you may notice some incorrect grammar or choice of words. Speakers are constantly searching for the right words under pressure, which explains some of the mistakes. As you read, try to understand the lines of argument that the two teams are giving. Try to create a flow sheet to follow the various arguments. Were all the points addressed? Which team did a better job of proving its side? Use your flow sheet to track the arguments and record which team did a better job. Compare your flow to the flow sheet at the end of the transcript.

You will find a brief explanation at the beginning of each speech. These explanations are from the *Teaching Notes* written by Alastair Endersby.[1] These explanations give you a preview of what you will read and help you to keep track of the arguments.

Prime Minister: Dan Neidle

Dan Neidle speaks for seven minutes in his Constructive speech. This fulfills the key responsibilities of the Prime Minister (PM) in the opening speech: outlining a clear case (with a straight link to the motion), providing some information on the case background, and presenting arguments that support the case.

The structure of the speech is as follows:

- Introduction: including a rhetorical opening and statement of the case in three parts
- Summary and division of arguments between himself and his partner
- Exposition of his first point. This begins with an explanation of how superpower rivalry in the Cold War actually led to stability and the avoidance of risk, in practice and in theory.

---

[1] Alastair Endersby, "We Felt Safer during the Cold War," *Teaching Notes*, On That Point DVD Series OTP0002, American format, British style Motion (New York: Open Society Institute, 2003).

- In the course of the speech, Dan takes two points of information, which are of different types:
- The first is literally a piece of information, a challenge about the application of game theory in the Cold War; Dan's response here is to clash at a factual level.
- The second point of information suggests a logical flaw in Dan's argument about the rationality of superpower leaders in the Cold War; a point he answers with an explanation of the doctrine of Mutually Assured Destruction. The issues raised in both points will resurface later in the debate.
- Then he moves to explain how nuclear weapons are more dangerous today than in the Cold War, both in the hands of rational leaders and in the possession of irrational states.
- Concluding summary of the arguments advanced in support of the case.

• • • • •

Prime Minister Constructive Speech (PMC) (7 minutes)
Mr. Chairman, ladies and gentlemen, members of this august house, I grew up in the 80s. I remember as a child dreading the nuclear threat. I remember the feeling that the Cold War was gonna be the death of us all. It was a feeling, though it wasn't just mine—it was a feeling that was shared throughout—the people marching in the streets, the people protesting with banners at Green and Common and in West Germany. Ladies and gentlemen, those feelings were strong at the time. But now, we can look back and we can say three things: we can say that the Cold War was actually not as dangerous as it seemed at the time. That with the benefit of historical hindsight looking back at the events which seemed so terrifying, in reality, they're only going to end one way. They're only going to end peacefully and without nuclear

holocaust. We can say, Mr. Chairman, that this wasn't just luck, but this was an inevitable theoretical result of the tensions of the frameworks with the technologies and with the politics of the Cold War.

And we can say, Mr. Chairman, something else. We can say that what the last few years have shown us beyond any doubt, is that the end of the Cold War has left us in a more dangerous world. That today, we're threatened—not only by states which seek to destroy us—but by individuals and groups and other non-state actors who are in a position of empowerment by technology and by politics, which they never were throughout the height of the Cold War. And Mr. Chairman, that is our case. I am going to talk about the states; I'm going to talk about Weapons of Mass Destruction, about Mutually Assured Destruction, and about game theory. And how that led, inexorably, to a position during the Cold War of stability between states, and that whilst it may have looked on the surface as though there was instability, beneath the surface, in fact, all was fairly safe. Mr. Chairman, my partner is going to look at non-state actors. He is going to show how the terrorist threat, whilst it may have existed during the Cold War, has since then risen to an entirely different level where now it actually threatens all of us—our lives and our economies. Mr. Chairman, my partner is also going to look at some of the events in the Cold War, which at the time seemed to have the potential to cause nuclear holocaust. And he's going to show that if you look at them with more than a superficial gaze, you'll see that actually the threat they involved was nothing more then superficial. Mr. Chairman, I'll turn first to the role of the states in the Cold War. And in the Cold War there were primarily only two states that mattered. There were two states maintaining a power balance—not just between themselves—but between their subordinate states, between their almost— empires. Now Mr. Chairman, we can see this because whenever any of their client states began to step out of line, it wasn't too long before America or the Soviet Union— whichever was supporting it—pushed them back into place. We can see that even in the case with the United Kingdom, which still had delusions of imperial grandeur in the 50s, until America told it during the Suez Crisis, that it could go this far and no further towards disturbing the stability of the world. We can see that in the case of Russia, which pulled China back from the brink during the end of the Korean War. We can see it in the case of Tanzania, when at the end of the Tanzanian invasion of Uganda, that the Soviet Union which stopped the Tanzanian occupation. Mr. Chairman, it was clear that the bi-polar state of the Cold War wasn't an accident. But that both states had a solid motivation to ensure that they were the only ones with the power to dominate on the world stage and they were the only ones to possess nuclear weapons. Now Mr. Chairman, nuclear weapons are really why this debate matters. Nuclear weapons, the element which enables a country on one side of the world to harm us here, and it's that more than anything else, which makes us feel less safe now than we did in the past. My colleague is going to talk about how nuclear weapons could, in the future, empower non-state actors. But it's clear in the hands of the state, nuclear weapons are far more dangerous today then they ever were during the Cold War. Now, the reason for this comes down to game theory and rationality and that ignoring the hype, ignoring the propaganda—-both sides in the Cold War had in their interests the maintenance of stability.

Point of Information:
It's interesting that you mention game theory. The founder of game theory, who was an advisor to the US government, was the very person who advised Roosevelt to start pre-emptive strikes against the Soviet Union after the Second World War as the logical outcome of applying game theory to the nuclear problem.

PM continues . . .
I don't think that's the case at all; I think you're referring to Teller who wasn't actually a founder of game theory whatsoever. I look forward to hearing that elaborated later on. I thought, Mr. Chairman, that the founder of game theory was John Von Neumann, who, I don't believe, had any contributions in that area whatsoever. But we look forward to a piece of revisionist history in fifteen minutes time.

Mr. Chairman, the difficulty now is that if you are a dictator of a small country in the Middle East and when you've seen what happened to the dictator of a similar country in Iraq, or to the rulers of a not dissimilar country in Afghanistan, clearly you need a way to protect yourself. You need a way to get yourself in the position where you cannot be invaded by a superpower. And there is only one way to do that. And that way is by the possession of nuclear weapons. A Russian leader knows the only way to maintain themselves in power, the only way to protect their regional hegemony is by the possession of nuclear weapons. And this isn't just a theoretical abstract. We've seen it in the case of North Korea. Compare and contrast North Korea and Iraq. Both led by unpleasant dictators, both oppressing their populations, both testing missiles, both threatening their neighbors, but America only threatened one. America only invaded one. It cannot invade the other and that is simply because of the possession of nuclear weapons. It sends, Mr. Chairman, not just a logical message but it sends a powerful political message to dictators across the world that the way forward, the way for them to protect themselves is by developing nuclear weapons. Now Mr. Chairman, the difficulty with this is, not only is it rational for them to possess nuclear weapons, but there are circumstances where it will be rational for them to use nuclear weapons. It will be rational for them to use nuclear weapons in defending themselves against any attempted intervention by the likes of America, but also defending themselves in regional conflicts. We can see that it would be rational for Israel to use nuclear weapons if it was attacked by the Arab states. It would be rational for Iran to use nuclear weapons if it was attacked by Iraq. It would be rational for India to use nuclear weapons against Pakistan, maybe even more rational for Pakistan to attack India before India can match its far superior army against Pakistan's. And Mr. Chairman, rational states with nuclear weapons are dangerous now to an extent they never were during the

Cold War. But irrational states, Mr. Chairman, are even more of a danger. North Korea—I put it to you, we don't know enough about its internal government to know if it is a rational or an irrational actor. But if indeed, the leader of North Korea is as bonkers as he appears to be, and he is irrational . . . then there could be any conceivable scenario by [which] he feels threatened by negotiations with the United States—at which point, he decides to use nuclear weapons. And North Korea . . . Yes sir.

Point of Information:
I'd be interested to know what particular things in the Cold War guaranteed that the leaders of the superpowers were actually rational minds?

PM continues . . .
The reason which guaranteed stability during the Cold War was Mutually Assured Destruction. It was the knowledge [that] the launch of one nuclear weapon, by one leader, of one superpower, or no matter how small of scale it was would inextricably lead to a snowball effect to the use of greater nuclear weapons—perhaps within Europe, perhaps on a tactical scale, and then on a greater scale throughout an exchange of intercontinental ballistic missiles and nuclear exchanges on the world level. And Mr. Chairman, that's the point on which my colleague is going to go into more detail. But at this point I'll simply summarize our case. Is that the world is a more dangerous place, it's a more dangerous place because of the absence of two powers and the stability they brought. It's a more dangerous place because the

increasing number of small powers that are empowered by nuclear weapons and non-state actors who are able to get nuclear weapons and other weapons of mass destruction and threaten our safety. And for that reason, Mr. Chairman, I beg to propose. Thank you.

Leader of the Opposition: Rob Weekes

He has no need to object to the case outlined by the Government (e.g., on grounds of tightness or specific knowledge), so this aspect of an LOC is demonstrated here.

The structure of the speech is as follows:

- Rob opens with an attack on the quality of the Government's case
- He proceeds to rebuttal of the Government's arguments
- He then outlines three constructive arguments for the Opposition
- Argument 1 is explained
- Argument 2 is explained
- Argument 3 is explained
- Rob concludes with a clear summary of the opposition's arguments.
- In the course of the speech he takes three points of information which challenge him in different ways:
- The first is an attempt to challenge Rob's analysis of events, arguing there is no difference between violent situations during the Cold War and since it has ended. Rob answers this by making a distinction between different types of conflict.

- The second responds to a direct challenge that Rob himself posed to the Government, in terms of a question which Dan answers. Unsurprisingly, given the way he set this point up, Rob answers it confidently and quickly.

- The third point of information challenges Rob to substantiate an assertion which he has just made. He answers it by providing several examples.

- Although speakers are often advised to take only two points of information, Rob shows that three can be taken without disrupting the speech, providing the answers are succinct and effective.

• • • • •

Leader of the Opposition Constructive Speech (LOC)
(8 minutes)

Well ladies and gentlemen, I know that on behalf of the side Opposition in this debate, it is standard to begin by thanking the Proposition for the splendid speech that they gave. But, unfortunately ladies and gentlemen, given the standing of the speech, I'm going to move straight into analyzing the two enormous arguments that we were presented. The first one was rather incredible; it was called the "states argument," rather ironically for this form of debate. And that was there were only two states of significance in the Cold War, presumably the United States and the USSR. And because there were only two states of significance, everybody felt safer. Presumably if you were American, you looked to America. If you were non-American and Communist, you looked towards Russia. Well ladies and gentlemen, we contest immediately that there were only two states of significance during the Cold War. What we would say straight out is millions of people died in the Cold War outside of those two states. Millions of people died in Vietnam. Millions of people died in Korea. Millions of people died in the Afghanistan conflict, millions of people died in the various Middle East conflagrations. And ladies and gentlemen—it's not good enough for the 1st Proposition to stand up and say, when we talk about safety, we're presumably meaning only the safety of Americans. We say no. Though the people who didn't feel safe during the Cold War were those people in the client states, in the proxy states who were significant because they were being killed. And it doesn't matter whether they're being killed by two states or different states. They lost their lives.

Point of Information:
Aren't there still people dying in, for example, Rwanda after that period? There's no change you can point to which makes your situation more dangerous.

LO continues . . .
Well, absolutely—there is. Because there is a significant difference between the situation which you had in the Cold War where you had a series of hot wars, not cold wars— where people were killed. And the situation that you have prevailing today where you have fewer conflicts and fewer people dying overall. As I point out obviously, the Rwanda conflict was a civil war, rather than the problem in the Cold War, which was a series of hot wars between different states. Now the second argument we are presented with was another extraordinary one—it was the nuclear weapons argument. Now, this was fascinating because if we have

nuclear weapons today, only we have a greater proliferation of them. And Dan apparently argued that because there's more nuclear weapons today, everything is safer. Whereas before, that you were guaranteed to have rational behavior on behalf of two leaders. Now, on a point of information, Mr. Kidd stood up and said what's the guarantee that they would behave rationally and we received no answer to that. And we say, moreover, where is the guarantee that Mutually Assured Destruction can possibly work in any manner that's different when you have greater proliferation of weapons? Go ahead.

Point of Information:
Your proof is fifty years of two superpowers armed to the teeth failing to attack each other with nuclear weapons. That's your proof.

LO continues . . .
And the present situation today is people still don't attack each other with nuclear weapons, even though there is more proliferation. So ladies and gentlemen, what I want to look at is this debate on three different planes. What I want to talk about firstly is the situation of the individual vs. the state. That's the terrorism situation. Secondly, I want to look at the situation of the state vs. the state—that's the war situation, and I've already said that that's the situation you had during the Cold War where millions of people were dying because of state-on-state conflicts, though generally there's much fewer people dying today in that type of situation.

And thirdly and crucially, I want to look at the situation of the state vs. the individual. And what do I mean by that? I mean huge state apparatus designed to persecute, intimidate and execute, exterminate individuals within the state. I'm talking about Stalinism; I'm talking about the Chizhevsky regime. I'm talking about Pol Pot in year zero. I'm talking about the people who died throughout the communist block because of the internal state situation.

So, first of all—individual vs. the state. This is the terrorism argument and it's one that Dan flagged but refused to address in his speech. And what we say is today, ladies and gentlemen, you have a terrorist threat, just as you had a terrorist threat before, ladies and gentlemen, but the difference is now, you have a terrorist threat which is situated where you have . . . Go ahead.

Point of Information:
Can you name a large scale targeting of civilians by terrorists during the Cold War?

LO continues . . .
What I can say is during the Cold War we had the Basque conflict, the conflict in Palestine, the IRA conflict. All those conflicts were still ongoing—there is no qualitative difference. The terrorist threat has existed throughout; it's simply an argument which can't fall on your side of the house.

So, the second point is the state's point. State vs. state war. And we said millions died in the Cold War and moreover millions of people were absolutely terrified during the Cold War. And we say things like the Cuban Missile Crisis was a point in which 75 percent of people believed they were brought to the brink of war. Now Seth can shake his head and say that didn't happen—obviously we didn't have a nuclear war then, but this is ultimately a debate which depends on a subjective feeling. We assert that people couldn't have felt safer during the Cold War, you assert otherwise. And we just simply say that given that 75 percent of people according to the surveys suggest that they felt that way, then that's all we need to actually say. And we moreover say that the same weapons exist today as existed during the Cold War. So given that those weapons existed, you can't possibly say that you feel less safe today, because if you have exactly the same weapons which pre-existed, as you have now.

And the third situation is the one I want to concentrate on, which is about the state vs. the individual. And that's about totalitarianism, ladies and gentlemen. And we say it's all very well that Seth is going to stand up and complain about individual terror groups and people feeling terrorized by individuals, small groups of people who are statistically insignificant in numbers they actually kill. Whereas what you should look at is the millions of people who were killed by much more organized terror groups that was the state itself. There was a Chizhevsky regime, there was the regimes throughout the communist block and now this is very important because it's not simply an argument bluntly about how many people died. Although let's get it clear, lots and lots of people did die. It's also an argument about accountability. Because what you fail to realize is that nowadays you have massive accountability that you didn't have before.

How do you have that? First of all, you have it through an international security system, a security system which is not only military but is also political. You have international tribunals that actually can hold people accountable for the degradations they commit against their own citizens and the citizens of other countries. You have even an International Criminal Court set up precisely to deter further human rights violations. The very concept of human rights has taken off massively since the end of the Cold War. And moreover you have accountability in the sense of the news media. Because it is a crucial part of our case, though we say nowadays you can quantify the threat. Nowadays, CNN can be in Tehran and say, "No, there is rational discourse in Iran. There are people who are prepared to listen to western ideas of debate. They're not rabid fundamentalists, ladies and gentlemen." And we contest that you couldn't possibly have said that before. You couldn't possibly have made the same arguments because you didn't have the information. So what we say very simply is the freedom of information allows people to know they are not at risk.

So what have we told you today? We've looked at three different planes. We've told you that many of the threats that're proposed by the Proposition are identical today, and we said that what's more, today you have much better systems of accountability and information that allow you to know that, in fact, you were less safe during the Cold War. And on that I beg to oppose.

Member of the Government Constructive: Seb Isaac

Seb Isaac delivers the eight-minute Member of the Government (MG) Constructive. This shows the use of rebuttal to defend the Government's arguments from the attacks of the Leader of the Opposition, and to attack the independent arguments put forward by the Opposition. It also features additional constructive material in support of the Government's case.

The structure of the speech is as follows:
- A brief introductory attack on one of the last arguments of the Leader of the Opposition
- A new constructive argument in three parts
- A defense of the arguments put forward in the Prime Minister's Constructive
- An attack on arguments put forward by the Leader of the Opposition

Seb takes one point of information, which is phrased as an attempt to clarify his argument but done in a manner designed to make his case look foolish. He handles it well by correcting his challenger's pretended misperception.

•••••

Member of the Government Constructive (MGC) (8 minutes)

Well, Mr. Speaker, Ladies and Gentlemen, I'm going to open my speech by looking at terrorism because that's really where Rob set a lot of his case. And he made this claim that because terrorism existed during the Cold War, terrorism can't be worse now than it was during the Cold War because terrorism is terrorism. Now taking that argument to its logical conclusion, we can go back to Hereward the

Wake, ladies and gentlemen, and say that Norman Britain couldn't possibly be a more or less vulnerable place to terrorism than it is—the modern world is. And that would make no sense. What we're arguing on our side of the house is not that terrorism has either disappeared or come into existence, we've argued that there's something qualitatively different about the Basque conflict that Rob pointed to and modern terrorism, ladies and gentlemen. And I'm going to point to three key reasons why that is.

The first is because at the moment what we have is acephalous rather than state-sponsored terrorism, ladies and gentlemen. And that's absolutely vital in understanding how and why terrorist organizations behave as they do now. Because there is an uncontrollability which was not the case during the Cold War. Because there has been a failure of sovereignty as a basic guarantee of certain minimal standards of behavior because ultimately during an era of state-sponsored terrorism, someone could be held accountable. And what we see during the Afghanistan and Iraq wars of today is precisely an attempt by the American government to shoehorn what is a qualitatively different type of terrorism into the old model of state responsibility in order to make it more easy to control. Because, as Kalschmidt has always told us, "War without borders is the worst thing that can possibly happen to our state," ladies and gentlemen.

But second what we look to is the very fact of state failure as a basis of terrorism. And state failure has been explicitly and obviously a product of the breaking up of the Cold War freezing effect, ladies and gentlemen. Precisely because there is no longer a stake in those unstable regions of the world and they have been allowed to collapse into the kind of situation we currently see in large parts of the Middle East, of Africa and of Southeast Asia in at this moment. And we show you that this not only gives a training and geographical base for terrorists, which wasn't available without state sponsorship before the failure of those states. And not only does it give many states and many groups of people a cause for terrorism which they did not have during Cold War, they did not have when they were living in failed states, ladies and gentlemen. But third, we show you that this is explicitly a cause of—no thank you, Rob—explicitly a cause of weapons proliferation and this doesn't just mean nuclear proliferation, which I'm going to go onto as my third point—this means proliferation more generally of the kind of small arms, the kind of explosives, the kind of airplanes, the kind of weapons facilities which are vital to a non-state actor capable of threatening people without the controls which were characteristic of state-based terrorism.

And finally, we look to nuclear proliferation as a product of the break-up and failure of states. We look at the fact that a state like Pakistan, which is now a nuclear state, President Musharraf has made it clear that he simply is not in control, not only of large parts of his eastern border, but also of large parts of his military, ladies and gentlemen. And that is certainly the case in many parts of the Russian Empire and many parts of the former Russian Empire, where there is potential proliferation of nuclear weapons, which was not the case during the Cold War.

So what we have is not only a new type of terrorist who lacks the kind of moral and sovereign controls which was the case during the Cold War, but we also have a new type of weapon standing with those terrorists. And we say that makes terrorism not quantitatively different, Rob, but qualitatively different to the way it was during the Basque conflict. So you can't just say the Basque conflict's still going on, so terrorism is no different, because firstly the Basque conflict is still going on, and secondly, we have new terrorism, new danger. Go.

Point of Information:
So I accept, do I then, your assertion that terrorism is, of course, completely different because in the Cold War you had moral terrorists and now you have amoral terrorists?

MG continues . . .
No, in the Cold War you had terrorists who were ultimately controlled by state actors who were subject to the epistemic pressures to conform and behave which were the case during a system of stable sovereignty, but which are not the case during the modern system. When you've read it, you can argue.

So ladies and gentlemen, let's look at this question of— Was Russia rational? Why was there Cold War stability? Well, I'll show you two things. Firstly, and it's worth noting, the high point of Cold War pressure was under Khrushchev and Brezhnev, not under Stalin—the person who you could most easily paint as an irrational actor, ladies and gentlemen. And Khrushchev and Brezhnev were explicitly rational in their behavior both within Russia and also and even more clearly in their external relations.

But secondly, that the pressures acting upon Russia and the USSR were systemic, rather than internal. So even if you'd had an irrational actor within the Kremlin, they would be unable and unwilling to behave in the irrational way that a state which is not subject to those constraints like North Korea, Iraq, Iran, Afghanistan, Pakistan—because of those systemic pressures. And I'll look to you at three examples.

The first and simplest is actually an argument from the epistemic community—the intellectual environment—because if we look at both the USSR and the United States during that period, what we see is that both of them were in the grip of realist political theory. The theory of people like Morgenthau and Waltz, the kind of people who preached explicitly about how to maintain sovereign borders, how to maintain sovereign power, how to maintain sovereign control. These are not people preaching about warfare; they're not people preaching about how to take over the world; these are preaching about how to stabilize your state.

And secondly we look specifically at the kind of crises, the Suez and the Congo, which we looked at in the first speech on our side of the house, and the fact that throughout those conflicts, there was the development of the architecture of United Nations peace keeping which both sides—the USSR and the United States—were heavily involved in precisely as a way of creating a get-out clause, a way of creating a pressure valve to take the pressure off themselves and the possibility of war out of those conflicts. They were explicitly involved in reducing the possibility of pressure.

And finally, we look at the one argument which might stand on your side of the house—the Cuban Missile Crisis. But the reason those weapons were put in Cuba, ladies and gentlemen, was precisely an attempt by Khrushchev to stabilize the situation, to stabilize the situation in a context where America had developed Intercontinental Ballistic Missile technology, which Russia could not without sparking a new arms race and without developing those missiles itself. And the moment it became apparent that that situation, that that act was potentially destabilizing rather than stabilizing he pulled back from the brink, as he always was going to. Because his intention was never to go to the brink. His intention was to allow himself so to do.

And finally, we look at Rob's argument about "people died in conflicts." And he said two things. Fewer people have died today. Well, I think the four million people who died in Rwanda in about six months would seek to disagree with you. But then when we put that to him, he said, "Well, but, that was civil war, not international war." And I say two things: Number one—go tell them that that means it doesn't matter, but number two, and more importantly, is it really true that the Vietnam conflict was not a civil war? Is it really true that the North Korean conflict was not a civil war? Are we really now claiming that these are, weren't in any sense one country before the war started? Just because you divide it at the end, doesn't mean it's not a civil war,

Rob. That's what happens sometimes when two equally matched sides fight a civil war. And finally, we look at this question of internal damage and I'll show you only one example, the example of Chechnya, because Rob said, "Oh well, now we've got an international criminal court and now that we've got accountable states and media, no one could possibly kick the hell out of people that live on their land." And I tell you, well they're managing in Chechnya pretty damn well, Rob, and if you really think that a couple of CNN reporters going in is going to deal with that problem, then you've got another thing coming. Thank you very much. Down.

Member of the Opposition: Andy Kidd

Andy Kidd delivers the eight-minute Member of the Opposition (MO) Constructive, including within it a new Opposition argument and rebuttal responses to the Member of the Government speech which came before.

The speech is very clearly organized, with the structure flagged up in the introduction:

- Very brief introduction setting out the four points to be covered
- Argues point 1, which is largely rebuttal of the Prime Minister's arguments
- Argues point 2, rebutting the arguments of the Member of the Government

- Argues point 3, defending the arguments of the Leader of the Opposition
- Introduces new point
- There is additional rebuttal of new material from the Member of the Government's speech
- Concluding summary

Andy takes one point of information. This is interesting, as the challenge is that Andy's analysis does not account for some important examples—showing another way in which information can literally be used to undermine an argument.

• • • • •

Member of the Opposition Constructive (MOC) (8 minutes)

Thank you very much indeed, Mr. Speaker, ladies and gentlemen; it's my great pleasure to continue the case for the opposition side. There are four points I'd like to make in this speech. The first two really following on from the first proposition speech with its focus on the nuclear stalemate question. The first point I want to contend, is that it is, in fact, inevitable that nuclear weapons would never have been used in the Cold War. And the second point I want to contend is that it is somehow different and much less inevitable that they wouldn't be used now. The third point is an examination of the non-nuclear threats that we've heard both from my partner, Rob, and also further down the table on the proposition. And the last point I want to make is one about the spread of liberal democracy and international trade and the impact of that on stability in the global community.

So, the first point that I want to make is around this inevitability. And Mr. Neidle's speech was very clear that this was extremely important because he recognized that we did feel under threat during the Cold War, but points out the retrospectively subject to retrospective analysis using his particular brand of game theory. It turns out after all—it was inevitable that nuclear weapons would ever have been used and therefore there was actually nothing to fear. Well, the first point is—and I raised it in a point of information to him—is that there is no guarantee that the principal actors in these situations are always going to act rationally. He accepted that there's no guarantee that actors today will act rationally, and apart from describing very generically and without saying what they were, the existence of so-called systemic pressures that in the Cold War made people rational, he hasn't actually done anything to convince us that that is the case. He talked about game theory but he didn't talk about what game theory was. And I'll address the point that he encouraged me to develop in his speech which is that the person he talked about, John Von Neumann—and you can go and look this up—John Von Neumann was an advisor to President Roosevelt at the end of the Second World War and his advice was that the logical application of game theory of minimizing the maximum possible loss, the Minimax principle, when applied to the nuclear problem resulted in pre-emptive strike being the only logical solution. He not only advised Roosevelt of this on a regular basis, but persuaded the vice president at the time that he was right.

Point of Information:
[Point of information was denied]

MO continues . . .
No thank you. And so, in the light of firstly that there can be no guarantee of rational behavior, and secondly that there are actually rational frameworks that suggest rational use of nuclear weapons during the Cold War, it is far from inevitable that nuclear weapons would never be used. And in fact that they were never used rests on many of the same controls that are still in place today. The principle one being that you are betting that anyone who has nuclear weapons is actually using them principally as a form of defense. And what we would argue on this side of the house is that that logic still holds true today, that the majority of people who have and are seeking to get nuclear weapons want them not as a way to launch a pre-emptive or offensive strike, they want them as a defense. They want them as a bargaining tool—no thank you—they want them for leverage but they do not want them to actually use them for the reasons that anyone who uses nuclear weapons—no thank you—faces dire consequences if they do and there is always more to be gained from not using them than there is from using them. And we would argue that no matter what threats of proliferation that side of the house put across, those fundamental principles still hold true. Yes.

Point of Information:
But that kind of analysis would not explain the deliberate efforts towards proliferation, which have been done by

exactly the states you came out acting only for defense for rational reasons.

MO continues . . .

No, no, I don't agree at all. I think that it gives states who feel under threat, particularly from countries like the US a feeling of security, a feeling that you have some leverage— no thank you—against the US if they ever feel that they are threatened. But the primary role of such weapons is purely for defense and security of those countries. The third point then, though, is around these non-nuclear measures. I think the best that we could possibly say is that the nuclear threats are about the same today as they was, were during the Cold War but certainly not any greater. But it is the non-nuclear threats where this side of house, we really see that the key argument lies. And this lies principally in three areas. The first is around the potential for escalating regional conflict. And we've heard a lot of analysis so far of the fact that there was a war in Rwanda that four million people died in after the end of the Cold War. Our point in this side of the house is that because that was a civil war, the fact that the war occurred was not to do with the broader geopolitical environment. No thank you. And the country examples that that side of the house have tried to refute of Vietnam, Korea, Afghanistan, and so forth were everything to do with the broader geographical environment. They may have arisen as civil wars but the very fact—no thank you—that the broader geopolitical environment was—as it is—was, was what caused these wars to escalate into non-civil war conflict. The fact that American soldiers were fighting in Vietnam defines it as a non-civil war. It became a, it became a global conflict which escalated far more than it would have done if the two active superpowers had not been arming and engaging—no thank you—with the sides in that conflict and far more people died—no thank you—in Vietnam and Korea and in Afghanistan than would have died—no thank you—had those conflicts occurred in a different geopolitical environment. The second point then is around oppressive regimes. My partner has already mentioned that to take a very pro-western view of the situation discounts the great fear felt by many people in oppressive regimes both within the communist bloc and under—no thank you—and under its influence. And moreover not only did that oppression take place, but the international community was powerless to act. The Security Council was essentially completely disabled during the Cold War through the power of veto—no thank you—that the superpowers had, and that today what we see is that the proactive activities of a nation like the United States acting as a global superpower creates a stable framework within which, within which nations which potentially may be disruptive face strong logic to not be. My final point is this that the spread of liberal democracy that the new geopolitical environment has brought, the spread of international trade and liberalization, in fact, brings the logic of game theory onto our side. That the possibility for cooperative gains through the cooperation of nations through trade, through democracies acting in the interests of their citizens reduces greatly the likelihood of any conflict between states. The issue of terrorism as well, Mr. Speaker, is one that we've covered on this side of the house. There were clearly terror-ist organizations acting before the Cold War and of course, many non-geopolitical enablers like worldwide communica-tions have enabled terrorist organizations that operate in many states to arise, but that's not uniquely to do with the end of the Cold War and in fact, we can see that such ter-rorist organizations—no thank you, sir—would have been a significantly greater threat—no thank you—during the Cold War. To wrap up, Mr. Speaker, ladies and gentlemen, this side of the house, we've said four things. We've said that in fact we weren't as safe as Mr. Neidle would have us believe during the Cold War. We still face in the world today, we face, at very best you could say, similar risks to nuclear con-flict, that the non-nuclear environment is far safer and that this trend is set to continue through the widespread, wider spread of liberal democracy and trade. For that reason, Mr. Speaker, we beg to oppose.

Leader of the Opposition: Rob Weekes

In this four-minute speech, Rob attempts to summarize the debate into clear reasons for voting with the opposition, showing how these outweigh the arguments of the government. It is structured as follows:

- An opening section identifies and rebuts the key government assertions on sovereignty.
- The clash over terrorism is addressed.

- The opposition's constructive arguments about what has changed are summarized.
- A brief conclusion emphasizes what hasn't changed and what has changed.

· · · · ·

Leader of the Opposition Rebuttal (LOR) (4 minutes)

Well, ladies and gentlemen, as they say on the TV, welcome back. The proposition case we've been given today really came down to two words linked by another. Sebastian and Dan said, "Sovereignty equals stability." Now, what's in that? Well, ladies and gentlemen, in that is an assertion. First of all, that you buy the idea that having a state with secure borders means that you have internal stability, so you would feel safer during the Cold War, and secondly, that you have to accept the assertion that all the client states and the proxy states, which we identified right from the outset has been those states affected by Cold War conflicts which were the hot wars that took place throughout the Cold War, actually had any sovereignty. You have to accept that states like Afghanistan were sovereign, that states like Vietnam were sovereign, even if their territory was occupied by other states. And ladies and gentlemen, Sebastian tried to explain this by use of the words "epistemic" and "systemic." Apparently, you have epistemic and systemic pressures that ensured that sovereignty was an effective force in reducing conflict. And ladies and gentlemen, I don't think an assertion that there is some international system is good enough to carry the whole case. And Sebastian didn't think so either. So he fell back on the moral terrorist argument. This was that terrorists are inherently moral if they're sponsored by a state, but if they're sponsored by individuals within that state, they are no longer moral, they become amoral terrorists who are liable to wreak destruction on the rest of the world. And ladies and gentlemen, they never addressed the argument, and it's very important to leave one of the major arguments completely hanging in the air, they never addressed the argument that sovereignty never protected people in the states from their own governments, ladies and gentlemen. Not even governments from their own dictators, from their own neighbors, ladies and gentlemen. They never addressed the fact that sovereignty was detrimental because a strong sovereign state meant it could persecute its own citizens with impunity. And ladies and gentlemen, what I said and what Mr. Kidd developed much more in his speech is, what has changed today? We say what has changed from the Cold War? Well, not the nuclear threat, we told you—the weapons are still there. It's still the same problem. Not terrorism. Terrorism is not a new fangled concept that came about, apparently as Sebastian argued by the collapse of communism. The state disputes about terrorism still exist today as they did before. No. What has changed? Are things like the flow of information which limits threats, which allows us to quantify threats. What has changed, as Mr. Kidd pointed out, was the level of international trade that binds people together so they do have a lot to lose if they're to engage in wars, ladies and gentlemen, or even to engage in terrorism. Where we were worried about China and Korea, now we're confident with China hosting the Olympics and being a member of the WTO. What has changed is the growth of liberal democracy. What has changed is the development of an international globalized objective news media, ladies and gentlemen, and not only a news media that is western, but a news media that is eastern as well and presents a different perspective, thereby allowing us to know—not just to feel safe, ladies and gentlemen, allowing us to have knowledge to enforce that feeling of safety. And what's also changed has been the development of international security organizations. So ultimately, ladies and gentlemen, what have we told you? We've told you what hasn't changed is the threats which have been identified by the proposition, but what has changed are all the trends in the opening of liberal democracy, accountability, and the flow of information. And on that, we beg very much to oppose.

Prime Minister: Dan Neidle

In this five-minute speech, Dan attempts to present the debate in terms of key issues that the government has won, showing how Opposition attacks and the Opposition's constructive arguments are unpersuasive. He includes direct rebuttal of new constructive material in the Member of the Opposition speech, which has not previously been responded to on the government side. The structure of the speech is as follows:

- An introductory attack on the nature of the Opposition's arguments with rebuttal of the first speaker
- Rebuttal of the new material in the Opposition's second speech

- A summary of the key issues in terms of what has changed and what has remained the same
- A brief final concluding summary

• • • • •

Prime Minister Rebuttal (PMR) (5 minutes)

Mr. Chairman, ladies and gentlemen, the Opposition have indeed been generous today, they've given us not just one opposition; they've given us two. They've given us an entirely new and different way of opposing a debate—at the start of Rob's first speech and again in his summation. It's a postmodern opposition, Mr. Chairman. It says ignore the facts, ignore the realities, ignore the dangers of nuclear war, ignore terrorism. What's important, Mr. Chairman, he says, is how you feel. What's important is that information is flowing across the world and we can understand each other more. Trade is flowing across the world, we can buy carpets cheaper. All of this he thinks makes us feel safer. And because of this we should ignore all the arguments about game theory, all the arguments about weapons of mass destruction, all the arguments about terrorism. All of these, Mr. Chairman, fly straight out the window because Mr. Weekes feels safe. Because Mr. Weekes likes listening to Aljezeera. Mr. Chairman, this is not an Opposition strategy. Mr. Chairman, I think that was recognized by the second speaker who suddenly got all technical on us and he decided that he could rule out half of our case by looking at examples like Rwanda, like the other examples of internal strife which we gave which had happened since the Cold War, and he could say that these were not relevant. That these were not part of the proposition case because he said they were not geo-political. These are special, these are different, and they don't count. But Mr. Chairman, he can still point to internal repression during the Cold War, he can still point to the Gulags, he could point to Stalin, he could point to Year Zero in Cambodia—this could count. It's easy, Mr. Chairman, by an incredibly complicated technical analysis the Opposition have proved that all of our arguments simply can't work, and all of their arguments automatically work. It's brilliant, Mr. Chairman, and it almost wins. Except for the tiny flaw that it lacks a scintilla of logic. It lacks a scintilla of argument to take us from the one to the other. Mr. Chairman, the key to this debate is very simple. It's to look at what has changed since the end of the Cold War and what has remained the same. And what's been clear throughout my speech and throughout my partner's speech is that an awful lot has remained the same. Liberation terrorism in the Basque region, in Ireland—it was there, it's still there. Internal state oppression, it was there during China, it was there a few years ago post-Cold War in Rwanda. Civil war, the disintegration of states, it was there during the Cold War in Korea and Vietnam, it was there afterwards, throughout Africa today, throughout Yugoslavia a few years ago. The Middle East, they give us the Yom Kippur War, we give them the Gulf Wars—we give them two Gulf Wars. Mr. Chairman, Tony Blair has declared war five times since 1997. Five times. No other British Prime Minister has within that period declared war even twice. And yet, they're telling us that the world is a more dangerous place during the

Cold War then it is today. Mr. Chairman, it simply doesn't work. No matter which way you add it up, no matter what kind of logical guillotine, you're caught between one and the other; the fact is that all these things have remained the same or have got worse since the end of the Cold War. So much, Mr. Chairman, for the differences, but Mr. Chairman, look very carefully at what's fundamentally changed—what was fundamentally misunderstood by both of the opposition speeches is the difference between a power balance between two states, and the multi-polar chaos that we see today. Because it wasn't just the fact there were only two states that had nuclear weapons, and this was their misunderstanding. It's that there were systemic, political, and economic factors within those two states which tied the states and the leaders of those states, and the power structures, and the whole politics of those states towards stability. An American President would never going to condemn millions of his countrymen to death in a nuclear holocaust. The Russian Premier, who was really just an artifice of the Russian bureaucracy, was never going to condemn the rest of that bureaucracy and the entire socialist experiment to catastrophe. Mr. Chairman, they were into entirely different situations from a Saddam Hussein or a Kim il-Song. There simply is no comparison; it may be politically incorrect to say that a leader like Kim il-Song is irrational, and a leader like Khrushchev was rational, but Mr. Chairman, it's true. It's true if we look back at the history of the Cuban Missile Crisis, as said a few moments ago. And it's true because of those powerful systemic, economic, and political reasons. So, Mr. Chairman, we look at what's changed and we look at what's stayed the same. What's changed is there are more powers, dangerous powers, unstable powers, and powers with access to weapons, which are frightening beyond belief. What's stayed the same is that the world is still full of conflict, full of drama, full of mass murder on a huge scale, and Mr. Chairman, that's always been the case. But what has increased since the Cold War, what's immeasurably increased since the Cold War is the danger of imminent catastrophe for all of us. That, Mr. Chairman, is why we felt safer then, and that, Mr. Chairman, is why I beg to propose. Thank you.

End of Debate

Final Notes

Complete your flow sheet. Compare your flow sheet to the following flow sheet to see how well you have followed the arguments. Were all arguments answered? Who built a stronger case? Who do you think won the debate?

According to the judge's notes, the Government, or Proposition, side (Neidle and Isaac) won. It was the unanimous view of the three adjudicators that the Government side was the stronger of the two teams. However, all agreed that the decision was a fairly tight one. They also noted that the second half of the debate was significantly stronger in terms of content and, particularly, the level of analysis.[2]

---

[2] Andy Hume, Bob Dalrymple, and Richard Wilkins, *Written Adjudication*, OTP0002 American format, British style (New York: Open Society Institute, 2003).

DEBATE FLOW CHART

PMC	LOC	MGC
1. States – a) 2 states held power balance: US/USSR b) 2 states oversaw their client states & stopped conflict c) Only 2 actors to have nuclear weapons	1. People didn't feel safe during Cold War a) Client states—people died	1. Qualitative diff. of terrorism a) Individual sponsored b) State failure c) Small arms proliferation essential to non-state actors d) New terrorists have lack of moral control
2. Weapons – a) Small state actors more dangerous. Dictators b) Possession of nuclear weapons deters invasion c) Rational action can mean attacks today. Didn't during the Cold War	2. Greater proliferation of weapons does not = rational actors or greater stability	2. Was Russia rational? a) Pressures under Khrushchev b) Pressures systemic, not internal
3. MAD – a) Risk of one attack ending world stopped one from being launched	3. Individual vs. the State a) Terrorism is more massive now	3. Russia is stable a) Systemic—not internal pressures b) Cold War involved UN peacekeepers c) Cuban Missile Crisis—Russia did it in response to ICBM's to create stability
	4. State vs. State a) Millions died in Cold War b) 75% believed nuclear war would happen—Cuban Missile Crisis	4. People dying a) Rwanda is a civil conflict b) Media just shows brutality—doesn't stop
	5. State vs. Individual a) Millions died at hand of state b) Totalitarianism c) Int'l security system d) Accountability e) Mass media	

MOC	LOR	PMR
1. Inevitabilty a) Not proven. Nuclear weapons would never have been used b) Minimax principle Preempt w/FDR c) No guarantee of rational behavior	1. Moral terrorist argument is flawed	1. Post-modern opposition a) Debate about how you feel b) Flow of info hasn't made us safer
2. Non-nuclear threats a) Regional—Rwanda, Viet Nam, N. Korea b) Oppressive regimes—UN powerless	2. They never answered the argument that people in sovereign states are oppressed by their own government	2. Oppositional strategy doesn't make our arguments invalid
3. Terrorism	3. Nothing has changed a) Nuclear weapons still here b) Flow of trade limits threats c) International stability d) Accountability e) Globalized news media—western and eastern	3. What has changed a) Terrorism is still occurring b) Internal state oppression c) Civil wars rage
		4. Difference in power balance of 2 states and multi-polar chaos

Glossary of Debate Terms

[Thanks to Robert Trapp of Willamette University for his contributions to this glossary.]

Abbreviate
See Shorthand.

Accident
The opposite of a hasty generalization. A fallacy that asserts that something generally considered true applies to all of the examples.

Adapting
Trying to debate in a way that pleases the judge.

Ad hominem attack (Attack on the person)
An attack on the debater, not the argument. This type of attack can also be used to attack someone for the group she belongs to.

Advantage
The part of the affirmative's policy case that demonstrates the positive effects of the affirmative's plan.

Affirmative
The side or team in a debate that supports the resolution.

Agent of action
When explaining a plan of action, this describes who will perform the action.

Amphiboly
A statement in which faulty grammar confuses the situation.

Analogy
An argument that supports associations between things based on their similarity or dissimilarity.

Analysis
When you make statements to show how the facts are connected to the claim or provide the reasoning for your arguments. Also called a warrant.

Appeal to authority
A fallacious argument that occurs when a person's opinion of something is considered the last word without allowing an argument against it.

Appeal to the people
A fallacious argument that occurs when a debater uses the popularity of a person, product, or belief to justify a conclusion about that person, product, or belief.

Appropriate
What is the most suitable or fitting for the time and place.

Argument
A controversial statement, frequently called a claim, supported by grounds (evidence) and a warrant. The standards of a logically good argument are acceptability, relevance, and sufficiency.
See also Standard of acceptability, Standard of relevance, Standard of sufficiency.

Argument construction
The process of creating an argument that occurs when you are "making" an argument for or against some viewpoint.

Articulate
To pronounce or say words clearly and slowly.

Assertion
A point in an argument.

Authority
An argument that supports a claim with the opinions of experts in the field.

Ballot
A sheet of paper on which the judge records the decision (who won the debate), the reasons for the decision (why that team won), and speaker points awarded to each debater.

Begging the question
A fallacy of acceptability that occurs when a debater introduces evidence that is the same as the claim.

Brainstorming
A process of listing as many ideas on a topic as you can think of.

Brief
A legal term for a written, shortened version of an argument; arguments with evidence prepared in advance of a debate for quick reference.

Burden
What a team (usually the affirmative but not always) must do to prove its case and win the debate.

Burden of proof
The requirement to provide evidence to support a claim.

Burden of refutation
The requirement to provide an argument against an argument advanced by the other team.

Burden of rejoinder
The requirement to provide the latest argument in a chain of arguments.

Case
One or more arguments sufficient to support a proposition.

Case argument
When the affirmative presents their arguments to accept the proposition.

Cause-effect argument
In a refutation against an off-case argument, this is a type of disadvantage. The plan is the cause; the effect is the negative impact of the argument.

Circular definition
A definition in which a term is defined by using the same term.

Claim
A controversial statement an arguer supports using reason. Claims can be fact claims, policy claims, or value claims.

Clash
Directly answering the other team's argument in a debate.

Complex statement
A proposition where more than one thing needs to be proved.

Con
The two person negative team in Public Forum debate.

Constructive criticism
To make comments about a performance in a positive way to motivate and educate.

Constructive speech
A speech that presents a debater's basic arguments for or against a resolution; new arguments are allowed.

Contentions
See Observations.

Context
The words, phrases, or passages that come before and after a word in a speech that helps to explain its meaning.

Contextual definition
The specific definition for the value term considering the time, place, and context of the argument at hand.

Controversy
Another term for Public Forum debate. *See* Public Forum.

Correlation
A false cause fallacy is an argument that incorrectly contends that two things are causally related when in fact they are not linked but simply related to a third thing that caused them both.

Counter-case
A case presented by the negative to respond to the affirmative.

Counter-contentions or counter-observations
The negative's specific points in their counter-case.

Counter-plan
A plan proposed by the negative team as an alternative to the affirmative plan.

Counter-point
Given when a debater asserts a point without providing evidence and the other side asserts the opposite.

Credibility
Something you have when the audience thinks you know what you are talking about.

Criteria
Something that must be proven to win; the most important values or standards in a debate.

Critical listener
A person who is able to listen carefully to what other people and the other team say and remember necessary bits of information.

Critical thinking
A process or skill that involves thinking about how you think. It is the process of asking and answering questions and trying to understand the process and reasons why you came to the conclusions that you did.

Critique
A judge's written comments on a ballot.

Cross-examination
A period during the debate when a member of one team asks questions of a member of the opposing team.

Crossfire
A part of Public Forum debate when both teams are allowed to question each other in a brief period of time.

Debate
The process of arguing about claims in situations where a judge must decide the outcome.

Debate format
The arrangement of a debate with rules establishing time limits, speaking order, and manner in which a debate will be conducted. Various formats of debate exist, each with its own way of debating.

Decision
The win or loss given by a judge in a debate; speaker points for each debate may also be part of the decision.

Decision rule
To provide for the judge a way to weigh the round and decide who won the debate.

Direct quotation
To read evidence word for word to support a claim.

Direct refutation
A refutation in which you point out the flaws in the opponent's argument.

Disadvantage
The harm that will come from a plan.

Disclaimer
A statement in which the speaker denies responsibility or connection.

Discourse
Discussion.

Divisions
Categories in a competition such as novice, junior, or open.

e.g.
For example.

Enforcement
In describing a plan, the person or agent who will make sure the plan is carried out.

Equivocation
A fallacy of language that occurs when a word is used in two different ways and the meaning of the word shifts during the argument.

Evidence
Different types of information (facts, statistics, theories, opinions, or narratives) that are used to support arguments; evidence can be divided into two categories: that relating to reality (facts, theories, and presumptions) and that relating to preference (values, value hierarchies, and value categories).

Expert opinion
Evidence given to support a claim from a source that has credibility because of education, study, research, or experience in the field.

Facts (evidence)
Observed or observable data.

Fair ground
When the proposition has enough arguments on both sides so that the debate is fair.

Fallacy
An argument that does not have good reasoning and that fails to meet any one of the standards of acceptability, relevance, or sufficiency.

False analogy
All analogies are false analogies, as they provide no warrants or evidence to support a claim.

False cause
A fallacy involving warrants; includes post-hoc fallacies and correlations. *See also* Post-hoc fallacies; Correlations.

Fight or flight response
A response dating from our ancestors who had to protect themselves from wild animals by fighting or running away. In modern times your brain thinks a speaking situation is a dangerous situation, so your body tries to find a way to increase

your strength through a faster heartbeat, increased oxygen in the body, and anxious movements.

Financing
The method of paying for a proposed plan.

Flow/Flowing
When you write down the arguments in a debate.

Flow sheet
Notes taken during a debate, usually written in columns so that arguments from each team can be written next to each other and can flow across the page.

Format
The speaking positions and times in a debate.

Funding
See Financing.

Gives a win
The process of a judge deciding who did a better job of debating.

Government
The proposition or opposition side of a debate. Is also referred to as gov.

Government team
The team affirming the resolution in a Parliamentary Debate. Also called the gov.

Grounds
See Evidence.

Grouping
To answer a set of arguments with one or more arguments rather than a line-by-line refutation.

Harm
A problem that currently exists in the status quo because of attitudes or laws that permit it.

Hasty generalization
A fallacy of reasoning whereby a conclusion is based on one or a few examples that may be too few or not like the rest of the larger group being discussed.

Highest Value
The minimal value at which a condition is acceptable.

i.e.
That is.

Impact
To explain why an argument is important.

Implied warrant
Unstated reasoning process that explains the relationship between the evidence and the claim.

Impromptu speaking
When you speak with little to no preparation time.

Inherency
Attitudes or laws that allow a condition (harm) to exist; the cause of the problem.

Invalid
A wrong statement of measurement.

Invitational tournaments
Tournaments in which debate teams participate by invitation.

Judge
An observer of a debate who has the responsibility of deciding which team has done a better job of debating.

Junior
An experienced debater who is no longer a novice but has not won at the junior level.

Jurisdiction
Authority.

Karl Popper Debate
A debate format that matches two three-person teams against each other: one team affirming the proposition and the other team

opposing it; each team has one constructive speech presenting its basic arguments for and against the proposition and two constructive speeches refuting the opposing team's arguments and summarizing its own.

Last shot
The final one-minute speech allowed by both sides in a Public Forum debate.

Lay judge
A judge who has never seen a debate before or is not an expert debate judge.

Leader of the opposition
The first oppositional speaker in Parliamentary Debate.

Lincoln–Douglas Debate
This debate format has only one person on a team (affirmative or negative). The same topic can be debated throughout the year. In college, a policy topic is used, whereas in high school a separate value topic is debated.

Linear
The presentation of something in a straight line. The linear way of organizing means that you present one idea after another in a specific way so that the audience can follow the line of ideas you are using to prove your arguments.

Line-by-line refutation
When a team refutes every point in the opponent's case.

Mandate
The specific action a plan requires.

Member of the government
The affirmative speaker who speaks after the Leader of the Opposition in Parliamentary Debate.

Member of the opposition
The negative speaker who speaks after the Member of the Government in Parliamentary Debate.

Monotone
A manner of speaking in which everything sounds the same.

Moot
When it is still uncertain who will win the argument.

Motion
A topic of argument.

Narrative
A way of presenting information by telling a story in your own words.

Need
The part of the affirmative case about policies that identifies a certain problem in the status quo that the existing system cannot solve.

Negative
The side in a debate that rejects the resolution.

Non sequitur
This general term is used when anyone provides an argument in which the claim or conclusion does not follow from the reasoning or grounds provided.

Novice
A beginning debater, usually having debated less than 30 rounds or not won a tournament.

Objective statement
A statement involving something that can be proved by observable phenomena or measurable facts.

Objective verification
This occurs when we make a statement and then have some agreed measurement to prove the truth of that statement.

Observations
Specific points addressed in a debate.

Off-case argument
Negative argument against a plan that would have its own organization, usually flowed on separate paper from the case.

On-case Argument
Negative argument against the issues that were defended in the first affirmative speech.

Open debater
A debater with the highest level of experience in tournaments, separate from the novice and junior divisions. Anyone can compete as an open debater, even a novice, but it is generally harder for a novice to win as an open debater.

Opponent
The term used for the other team, regardless of what side you are debating.

Opposition
The team negating the propositional team in Parliamentary Debate.

Oral
Spoken, not written.

Oral critique
The judge's oral explanation of the decision right after the debate.

Outlining
Writing notes in an organized way.

Oxford-style debate
A version of policy debate in which no cross-examination is allowed.

Paraphrasing
Explaining evidence in your own words.

Parliamentary Debate—NPDA
A debate format in which the two teams take on the role of governmental leaders. This format requires a different topic for every round.

Parliamentary Debate—World's Style or European/British Parliament
A version of Parliamentary Debate in which four teams compete at the same time: two teams on the propositional side and two teams on the oppositional side.

People skills
The ability to talk to others with ease.

Perspective taking
Role playing to present the best arguments for an issue.

Plan
A course of action proposed by the affirmative when debating a proposition of policy intended to solve the problems identified by the "need" or "harm" arguments.

Planks
The individual points of a plan, which include the agent of action, the mandates, financing, and enforcement.

Point
A significant, outstanding, or effective idea, argument, or suggestion; an assertion.

Point not well taken
When a team calls for a point of order and the judge decides to allow the argument to stay in the round.

Point of information
To seek permission to interrupt the speaker for the purpose of asking a question or clarifying or making a point during a Parliamentary Debate.

Point of order
To interrupt a speaker in a rebuttal speech to ask the judge to make a decision about whether a new argument was offered in a rebuttal speech.

Point well taken
When a team calls for a point of order and the judge decides that it is a new argument and does not allow the argument.

Policy Debate
A debate format in which opponents debate a policy (usually a governmental policy) currently in effect. Typically debaters have the same topic for the entire school year and read evidence, word for word.

Post hoc fallacy
Occurs when a debater assumes that because one thing happens before another, the first must have caused the second.

Preliminary rounds
The beginning rounds in a tournament before the elimination rounds. All teams compete in the preliminary rounds. Six preliminary rounds are standard for most tournaments in the United States.

Preparation time
The time allotted to each team for preparation during the debate (eight minutes in Karl Popper Debate).

Presumption
The assumption that current policies will be maintained until someone makes a case that another policy is a better option.

Presumption (evidence)
A statement concerning what people ordinarily expect to happen in the course of normal events.

Prima facie
Latin for "on first face"; a requirement of cases presented that means that all necessary issues are present.

Prime Minister
The first propositional speaker in Parliamentary Debate.

Pro
The two-person affirmative team in Public Forum debate.

Proposition
A claim made by a debater and supported by a combination of claims: a statement to be proven (fact, value, or policy).

Propositional team
See Government team.

Proposition of fact
A statement that can be proven with some kind of a measurement.

Proposition of policy
A statement that makes a recommendation that a certain action should be taken.

Proposition of value
A statement that tries to prove an opinion.

Public Forum
A debate forum that is audience-oriented usually without expert debate judges allowed. Topics are new each month and are chosen for their balance of evaluative arguments on both sides. Evidence is encouraged but usually not read directly, and should be part of the decision by the judge.

Qualitative significance
This statement describes in words why a value is important in a debate.

Quantitative significance
This statement provides numerical or statistical evidence of why an issue is important in a debate.

Question-begging epithet
When an adjective or adverb is added to a term to form an additional argument.

Reasoning
The process used to connect evidence to a claim; providing reasons for something. *See also* Warrant.

Rebuttal speeches
The speeches in a debate that challenge and defend arguments introduced in the constructive speeches; no new arguments are allowed.

Recent, relevant, and reliable
Three tests for all evidence that examine the age of the evidence, whether the evidence proves a point, and whether the source can be trusted.

Red herring
A fallacious argument that shifts the focus from the original argument.

Refutation
The process of attacking and defending arguments.

Refute
To prove something wrong.

Rejoinder
An argument given, regarding the last argument of the other team, about why they are wrong, why you are right, and the impacts of your argument.

Research
The process of locating and selecting evidence in preparation for debate.

Resolution
A debate topic specifically worded to make for fair debates.

Resolutional analysis
An observation that provides the framework for the affirmative's case; it may include definition of terms, context, criteria, value, and decision rule.

Roadmap
A statement at the beginning of a speech letting everyone know the order of a debater's speech.

Rounds
When all of the teams are debating at the same time.

Shorthand
A system of writing that uses abbreviated words and symbols to rapidly record what is being said.

Significance
An issue that is important.

Signpost
To provide the order of the organization of the arguments to be presented.

Solvency
Arguments that explain why a plan will cure the harm.

Speech anxiety
Nervousness about speaking or giving a speech in public.

Standards
Means of evaluating a term or value accepted by all parties.

State your point
What a judge says when a team calls out, "point of order." When a judge calls for a team to state its point, then the team must explain why the argument from the other team was not mentioned in the constructive speeches and is therefore new.

Statistics
Evidence expressed in numbers.

Status quo
The course of action currently in use (i.e., the present system).

Stock issues
The main arguments necessary to prove a case; in Policy Debate the stock issues for the affirmative are need, significance, inherency, plan, and solvency.

Stop a harm
To prevent something bad from happening.

Straw argument
A fallacy that occurs when an arguer, intentionally or unintentionally, misinterprets an opponent's argument and then proceeds to refute the misinterpreted argument as if it were the opponent's actual argument.

Straw man
See Straw argument.

Style
The language, voice, and body language used by a debater.

Subjective opinion
A belief or attitude that cannot be proven and that is typically biased.

Taken under consideration
When a team calls for a point of order and the judge decides later if the argument is new or not.

Talking with your hands
The act of constantly moving your hands when you talk.

Tautology
See Circular definition.

Ted Turner Debate
See Public Forum.

Term
Word or phrase.

Testimonial
A statement in support of a fact or claim. An expert opinion.

Theory
A statement that explains other facts or that predicts the occurrence of events.

Thesis statement
At the beginning of a debate or speech, a statement given to let the audience know exactly what your speech is about. It consists of only one sentence to tell the audience the purpose: to inform, to persuade, or to entertain.

Threshold
The point in an argument at which you have provided enough evidence to prove your argument.

Tie goes to the negative
A term that means that it is best to stay with the status quo since the affirmative has not proven that its plan is better.

Topic
An area for discussion or debate.

Topicality
An instance where the affirmative team does not debate the resolution.

Toulmin Model
A model of argument developed by philosopher Stephen Toulmin. The basic model includes claim (statement), ground (evidence), and warrant (analysis).

Tournaments
A series of debates in which a number of teams or debaters compete to win.

Triad
Three main parts of an argument: claim, grounds, and warrant.

Valid
True or legitimate.

Value
Evidence based on the audience's preferred value.

Value case
A case supporting a proposition of value; three principal elements of such a case are describing, relating, and evaluating.

Violations
Ways that the other team has not met the standard of the topic.

Voting issue
An instance when the judge does not have jurisdiction or when a debater will summarize the winning arguments in a rebuttal speech.

Warrant
Stated or unstated reasoning process that explains the relationship between the evidence and the claim.